SOUL MATES

Also by Rita Rogers

REACHING FOR THE CHILDREN (WITH JOHN MANN)

FROM ONE WORLD TO ANOTHER

MYSTERIES

LEARNING TO LIVE AGAIN

SOUL MATES

A PRACTICAL, SPIRITUAL GUIDE TO FINDING TRUE LOVE

RITA ROGERS

PAN BOOKS

First 2000 by Pan Books
an imprint of Pan Macmillan Ltd
Pan Macmillan, 20 New Wharf Road, London N1 9RR
Basingstoke and Oxford
Associated companies throughout the world
www.panmacmillan.com

ISBN 0 330 39078 3

13 15 17 19 18 16 14 12

A CIP catalogue record for this book is available from the British Library.

Printed and bound in Great Britain by
Mackays of Chatham plc, Chatham, Kent

For

David, Denise, Louise, Scott, Danny, Benjamin,
Ashley, Charlene, Alesha, Molly and Lee David

Rita Rogers is a medium of Romany origin whose popularity and outreach has exploded not only since her first book was published, the bestselling *Reaching for the Children*, but as her reputation and the respect in which her work is held have grown. Mrs Rogers can be reached by writing to her at Mill Lane Farm, Mill Lane, Grassmoor, Chesterfield S42 5AD. She promises to read every letter she receives, but can only reply if a stamped, self-addressed envelope is enclosed.

All the stories included in this book are true, and all those featured have given their permission for their experiences to be reprinted. At their request, the names of some people in the case histories have been changed in order to respect their privacy.

Contents

Preface

I first met Rita Rogers in 1996 when I was writing an article for British *Vogue* about psychics and mediums. I had intended the piece to be a scathing attack on the psychic industry. Like many I had never really believed in mediums. They were, I thought, for people who had nothing better to do with their time or their money. No rational, logical person could believe that spirits spoke to people beyond the grave. In the course of my research I visited over thirty people who claimed to have 'psychic' powers but the information they offered, bland generalizations about my life, had done little to convince me.

The night before I was due to deliver my article someone suggested I contact Rita Rogers at her home in Derbyshire, England. I was told that she was good, so good that she had a two-year waiting list, one which boasted celebrity names. I was told that she could even give readings over the telephone because she was clairaudient – which means she heard voices in her head as well as being able to see things. And so that night, with some reluctance, I telephoned Rita and asked if she would read for me. This was one last chance for the 'industry' to redeem itself.

In truth, I doubted that she could tell me anything that would alter my views, or the shape of my article. But two hours later I found myself back at my computer rewriting my piece. Rita had challenged everything that I had held to be true about what she and her like did. A stranger, she had come up with details about my life – past, present and future – that no one, not even my family, could have possibly known.

Rita is of Romany origin, born in Nottinghamshire in 1941. She was the second daughter of a family of six and was raised in the mining town of Mansfield. Rita believes that she inherited her 'gift', along with a four-hundred-year-old ball, from her grandmother, Mary Alice Stringfellow, who was a Romany gypsy. Rita was always scared of her 'gift'. As a child, Rita was always hearing and seeing things – people, colours, images she did not understand. It terrified her. During her childhood years this gift would seem to cause her more problems than it did good. Her mother, who was not Romany, would chastise her for 'romancin''. 'It was a word I heard so often during those years I came to believe it myself,' she said.

The visions and voices that Rita experienced would not leave her, although for years she tried to suppress them. It was not until she was in her twenties that she came to understand what it was all about. Having tried and failed to fight it and live an ordinary life as a housewife and mother to her four daughters, she realized that she could no longer escape her destiny. In time she became aware that her psychic powers were not something to be frightened of, but that they could be used to help people. She spent the next ten years practising on friends and local people before turning professional.

Today Rita reads for eleven people a week. A reading can last anywhere between forty minutes and three hours. Her clients come from all over the world to see her; from Florida to Sydney, Johannesburg to Texas, people regularly descend on the tiny village of Lower Pilsley to meet with, what some have come to describe as, the world's greatest medium.

Over the years Rita's reputation has grown by a word of mouth basis. She does not advertise; she does not need to. Her waiting list is longer than ever, and indeed now finds it almost impossible to take on clients other then those with whom she has a long-term relationship or whom she reads in the course of her journalistic work. Her fee is still modest compared to most mediums, however, and more often than not she will refuse to accept any money from some of the people who come to see her for help if they are desperate and unable to afford the basic fee.

She has also read for a list of high profile clients to whom she has always remained discreet and loyal. In *From One World to Another*, she talked about the nature of her friendship with Diana, Princess of Wales. She has also worked alongside the police, being involved in solving several well-known murder and child abduction cases.

Through her friendship and working relationship with Diana, Princess of Wales, Rita gained worldwide notoriety. But she has earned praise from the media for her loyalty and discretion on the subject. Rita is, in fact, fiercely protective about all of her clients. Press her on the subject of her VIP client list and she will glare at you. '*You* spend an afternoon reading for a woman who has lost both children in a fire, or a young woman with breast cancer who knows that she is not going to live past her thirtieth birthday, and then tell me who the VIPs *really* are,' she says.

Anyone who knows Rita, or who has come into contact with her, will tell you what a remarkable woman she is, not least for her extraordinary and genuine gift but also because of the compassion and sympathy that she freely gives to all who come into her life. Her outlook and belief systems have brought comfort and hope to thousands of people across the world, not only through her readings but through her books, *Reaching for the Children* and *From One World to Another*, and columns and articles as well.

When Rita first read for me I was amazed by the detail she was able to give me about my life. She knew the names of people in my family who had passed away. She knew the date and circumstances of a friend's tragic death. She told me about my family, and what they did. She knew where I lived and what had happened to me. She told me about my personal relationships and predicted what would happen in the future. I did not believe all her prophecies at the time, many were just too incredible, too improbable. But over the past three years, one by one, each has come true, and I am no longer surprised by anything she tells me.

Natasha Garnett

Introduction

Finding true love is the most rewarding thing that can happen in anyone's life. However successful, happy or peaceful we are there will always be something missing from our lives until the moment we meet our soul mate. Whoever we are, whatever we do, whether we realize it yet or not, we are all searching for love. For love is the only thing that can ever bring spiritual and emotional fulfilment into our lives. Is it any wonder then that we spend so much of our adult lives trying to find it?

Every day I receive hundreds of letters and telephone calls from people all over the world. They come from different places, from different backgrounds, some are young, others old, and yet they all ask the same questions. 'Who is my soul mate?' 'When will I find them?' 'Is there anyone out there for me?' You see, not all of my work is with people who have lost someone; a lot of it is with people who are *looking* for someone.

I decided to write this book because as much as I wanted to I could not answer all these letters and calls personally. And yet I knew how important this subject was. I realized that it was important for people to understand that they could and would find true love eventually.

You see, whoever we are, wherever we are from, whatever we look like, we all have a soul mate, and somewhere out there they are waiting to meet us. We are destined to be together, and so destiny will bring us together.

*

I knew my destiny young. My grandmother, Mary Alice Stringfellow, told me when I was just eleven years old what my future held. Mary Alice was a Romany gypsy, who, at six foot two with her waist-length hair and her fierce tongue was a formidable character. She was a well-known psychic and a great believer in destiny.

As a child I spent many hours in her company learning about Romany ways and beliefs. She would tell me about the afterlife and how we would all become spirits. She explained to me that this life here was just one part of our whole lives, that our death was not the end, but a journey into the next world, a world that was spiritual and thus a better place to be. She told me that who we are is not what we see, but what lies within. She spoke of the eternal life of the soul. And she told me that we all had soul mates.

My grandmother had met her soul mate, my grandfather Herbert Stringfellow, under a hedge bottom in Nottinghamshire. Grandma Alice had been travelling south with her mother, walking barefoot, sleeping under barns and hedgerows, selling flowers and fortunes along the way. They had stopped in Nottinghamshire because her mother was ailing from the journey and could go no further. In taking shelter they met Grandpa Herbert, who was out walking. This, according to Grandmother Alice, was fate. And although at five foot two he was a foot shorter than she was, he was her soul mate.

As a child I heard this story many times, but it never bored me. I found my grandmother and her tales of destiny and spirit worlds mesmerizing. She would tell me how we all had a path to follow, and that the spirits had decided on this path before we were even born.

One afternoon Grandma Alice told me my path. She said that I would marry at sixteen, that I would have four girls and that three of them would be born on the same numerical date. She said that I would be widowed young, in my thirties, and that one day I would become well known for my work as a seer.

I did not believe any of this at the time. I had no intention of marrying young, or becoming a seer. I wanted to have a job, to become a nurse or something like that, and then one day start a family.

But as Grandmother predicted I did indeed marry young, in 1957 at the age of sixteen, to a coal fitter called Dennis Rogers. My daughters Pat, Mandy and Julie were born on the same numerical date. Kerry followed later. And when I was in my thirties Dennis was taken from me, after a battle with cancer of the bowel.

*

This book is about recognizing our destiny and understanding that we are all given a special person to love. In the following chapters I will discuss ways in which we can tell if we have found true love or not, how we can help ourselves find our soul mate, and what to do when you have. I will talk about learning to live with your soul mate, and how you can learn to live without them when they pass away. You'll read the true-life stories of people who've consulted me, reprinted with their permission. Many of them are touching; most of them are also humorous, because the world of spirit isn't all about doom and gloom, especially when you're talking about the joy a soul mate brings. But I hope you'll find all the stories reassuring.

You don't have to believe in spiritualism to use this book. But the most important thing you come to realize is that whatever you believe in, we all have a soul, and that true and everlasting love lies within our spiritual nature. Thus this is a spiritual guide to finding, recognizing and living with true love.

ONE
The Soul

WHAT IS A SOUL MATE?

Soul mates are two individuals who were destined to be together, for ever. We all have a soul mate, someone we have spent our lives waiting to meet, and with whom we hope we can eventually share our lives. And somewhere out there, there is someone who is waiting to be with you.

A soul mate is a special person with whom you are spiritually linked. Between you exists a bond that can never be broken. A bond of love and understanding that transcends everything: separation, tragedy and even the grave.

Between you and your soul mate exists an immutable law of attraction. It is like a magnetic force pulling us towards that special person, a force field from which we can never escape. The attraction we feel for our soul mate goes beyond anything we have felt before. Looks, age, sexuality, class or background all become irrelevant because the attraction for your soul mate is deeper and more meaningful. The attraction between you two is one of the soul.

Your soul mate is, therefore, someone who loves *you* and by that I mean all of you. It is not the way you look, the way you think, what clothes you wear. It is not because of your age, your job, and the friends you keep. Your soul mate is someone who loves you because you are you. They have looked beyond your appearance and all the things that other people might be attracted to, and fallen for who and what you really are. And from this deep, deep love of you comes an understanding that you will never know from another person.

Finding your soul mate will make your life complete and fulfilled. The feeling that something is missing from our lives disappears as soon as we meet them. For the love that we share with our soul mate enriches us, fulfils us and gives meaning to our lives, bringing us joy and happiness. Meeting your soul mate will make you feel whole. It is a love that makes you glad to be alive and not afraid to die.

Your soul mate was put on the earth for you. From the moment your spirit was conceived you were destined to be with another soul. You and your soul mate are put together to make each other's lives happier. It is one of the deepest and most profound loves we will ever experience.

Your soul mate may come from another place, another world even, but when you meet them none of that matters. You may even be opposites but you still feel that this person is right for you. You cannot believe that there is someone on this earth with whom you share so much.

A soul mate is someone who is perfect in our eyes. Other people may look at them and ask, 'What on earth do you see in them?' But in your eyes your soul mate is perfect. We rarely see faults in our soul mates and when we do we tend to overlook them because they have so many other attributes that we admire and because we love them so much. That does not mean that we idolize them or that we try to pretend that they are better than they are. When we meet our soul mates we love all of them. We accept their differences and imperfections just as we hope they accept the differences and imperfections in ourselves.

We feel this way about our soul mate because the love we have for them comes not just from our hearts but from deep within our souls. And it is for this reason that the love we have for our soul mate is different from any love we have known before, or will ever know again.

It is a love that comes from the very core of our being. It is a love that does not fade. It is a constant and unconditional love, a love shared by two people who are eternally bound together. It is mutual, unquestioning, trusting, pure and always true. It is a love that will shape your life, one that will give you strength. A love shared by two souls.

THE SOUL

The soul is the place where we are most true. It is, if you like, your spiritual blueprint. It is here that we keep our desires, our innermost needs and our instincts. It is our soul that determines how we really are, how we relate to others and ourselves. It is the place our emotions come from, our empathy, our sympathy, our love and our grief. Our soul is responsible for shaping our identity. It is the force behind our being. It is *you*.

The soul is a symbol of the spiritual and non-bodily aspect of individual human existence. It is a force that not only gives us life on earth but one that persists long after our deaths. The soul is immortal. Existing as a separate entity from our physical form, it is what we take into the afterlife and is what gives us life well after the grave. Therefore, the love we have for our soul mate is an eternal love, one that can survive anything – separation, misfortune, suffering and death.

In order to find true love then, you must not only open your heart but also your soul. To be in a position to find this love you must be prepared to look deep within yourself, to be willing to give all of you to another person, to let another person into the core of you.

Convention associates feelings of love with the traditional symbol of the heart. Both literature and art suggest that the emotion of love comes from the organ that gives us life. Hence these discourses are filled with images of pounding hearts, broken hearts, bleeding hearts and loving hearts. We think of this love emanating from deep within our breast. But true love goes deeper than that. True love is not found within the breast but within our essence, the immortal soul. We think of the heart as being vital to our lives. It is, but only to human life. The soul is vital to our eternal life.

However, when I am discussing the love between soul mates I do not like to use the heart as a symbol of this love. For although the heart is the one organ that is vital to life, when it stops beating it dies. It has a lifespan. The soul, on the other hand, is immortal. It existed before we came into this life and it will continue to do so long after we have gone.

Throughout our lives we will experience many kinds of different love. There are many loves that do come from the heart but there is only one love, that comes from the soul. You may have had relationships in the past that were full of love, passion and affection. You may be in such a relationship now. These relationships may have been intense but short-lived affairs, or they may have lasted for many, many years. You may love this person very much, you may even think that you are *in* love with them. But there is a great difference between an affair of the heart and one of the soul. It is the difference, if you like, between the physical and the spiritual.

The point I am trying to make is that you can stop loving a person whom you love with your heart. You may have feelings of love for them still, you may still like and be friends with them, but the real love has gone. This will never happen to you and your soul mate for the love that comes from deep within your soul never dies. Your soul mate might be separated from you. You may have only been together for a matter of weeks; you may never have the opportunity to see that person again while you live. They may have been taken from you, or have even died, but that love you have shared will never leave you. It will live on for eternity.

For, unlike the heart, which can be fickle, the soul is always constant. The love deep within your soul is eternal and unconditional. To find the truest love of all you must follow your soul, and not your heart. The emotions stirred when you love someone with your heart, such as passion, infatuation, rapture, will all diminish with time. But the feelings that come from the soul will never fade because they are the feelings that are truest to you. Your soul mate, after thirty years together, may not drive you to passionate distraction in the way they did when you were first together, but you will have other, greater, deeper feelings for them. The love between soul mates is constantly evolving and deepening.

This spiritual love comes from an understanding of another person and ourselves. What makes us fall for our soul mate and love them is the spiritual relationship we have with them. It is not about physical attraction, money or status. It is not about what we are on the outside but who we are within. Many people who have a certain 'type', such as dark men or fair women, for example, say that when they met their soul mate they were not the sort of person they normally would have gone for. Sometimes they are even the exact opposite of their type and they cannot really explain why they were attracted to that person. Nevertheless, they felt this pull, this magnetic force that drew them to that individual.

Why we feel this way towards our soul mates is that our spirits are drawn to each other. Because this love comes from our spirits nothing else matters. When we find our spiritual match the person we fall for could be a tramp and we wouldn't care. Once that connection is made nothing else matters to us.

SPIRITUAL LOVE IN A MATERIAL WORLD

Finding true and lasting happiness is about concentrating on the spiritual side of life as opposed to the material and physical side of life. Once you have found this kind of love you will feel richer and better off than any millionaire. As my Romany grandmother, Mary Alice, used to say, 'If you are happy and healthy, then you are wealthy.'

The world we live in today is a material one. We all want for more. We aspire to rich and glamorous lifestyles. We associate security with how much money we have in the bank. We think about comfort not in terms of whether we have a roof over our heads and a meal on the table but by how many cars we have in our driveway and how many holidays we can take a year. We measure a person by their job, their salary, and the clothes they wear.

Money and material goods can make our lives easier, it can take the stress and worry out of our routine existence and give us greater freedom, but it cannot make us better off as people. Through my readings I have come into contact with a great many rich, famous and beautiful people. To an outsider their lives might seem enviable. What could they possibly want for? They have everything. Well, if they did, then I am sure they would have better things to do than visit me.

You see, deep down we are all the same. Whether you are considered beautiful or plain, whether you are rich or poor, young or old, you are all ultimately looking, searching for the same thing in life – love and fulfilment. You may not even recognize it yet but it is true. You may think that winning the lottery will make your life better, that being a movie star will give you fulfilment. They won't. These things may even make your life easier, may make you happy, but it is not an eternal happiness.

A size eight does not have a better chance of finding a soul mate than a size sixteen. True love and a contented soul do not come free with a designer outfit or by being with the most physically attractive person in the room. Stocks and shares will not give you inner peace. All these things are transient. Looks, money, fame, reputations can all be lost. Spirituality, lasting happiness, eternal love are what we should all strive for and come from deep within.

I am talking about the attraction of materialism here because I think that in order to find the best kind of love and happiness in life we need to stop worrying about what we are like on the outside and concentrate on what we are within. I always say to people who wonder whether they are with the right person or not, 'What would you do if he was a tramp? Would you still feel the same way?' Honestly, a person who has met their soul mate can answer this question without hesitation!

Before we can truly find, recognize or enjoy life with our soul mate we must approach life with a spiritual aspect. You do not need to be a religious person to be spiritual. You do not have to even believe in an afterlife, or the existence of spirits. It is about getting away from the material. It is about understanding that you have a spirit and that you have a soul.

When we find spiritual love we no longer care about the material qualities: money, income status, the size of their house or whether they have a nice car. Thoughts and words between soul mates are what counts. They are more valuable than gifts.

Could you still be with this person if they lost all their money? It might change your life but if you were truly in love it would not change your relationship, your feelings for them. As my grandmother also used to say, 'Give me five years of happiness in a hut with someone I love, than forty years of drudgery in a mansion.' When we meet our soul mate we have no regard for money, means, income, status. These material things are not important for all we care about is being with them. We would happily go and live in a tent if only to be with this person.

I am always amazed by the strength of the power of love. Love has the ability to completely change people.

When we fall in love our priorities can alter overnight just because we have discovered fulfilment. I have known hard businessmen driven by power and money, people who are always working and on the move, give it all up for love. The thing that they were trying to find in money and power, which will never give total fulfilment anyway, they find in love. This is because whoever we are we all need love, we all need something more spiritual and more meaningful in our lives.

Some people I read for have in the past fallen in love with flattery, good looks and possessions, such as fancy cars and money. It is easy to do. These things tempt us, and attract us to a person by making their life, their personality, seem alluring. But these things do not last, which is why the relationship does not last. We are all looking for something more whether we recognize it or not. A woman who I read for regularly left her husband recently. He was good-looking, rich, and successful; she was fairly young and very attractive. She seemed to have it all – nice clothes, beautiful houses, servants and secretaries. She could go anywhere in the world she wanted, she didn't have to work and was rich enough not even to care about making any more money, for the money she had made money itself. But she was always looking for more and she was unhappy and bored. She tried many different ways of finding a meaning to her life but none of them worked. Eventually, she understood that the only way in which she could be happy again was to leave her husband. When she left she did not ask for a financial settlement. She had no children and did not want anything from her husband. Her friends thought she was mad but I don't think she was. The fact is she knew that the money and the lifestyle did not give any meaning to her life. To find a purpose and eventual happiness, she knew she would have to escape from that world and start doing something for herself. She is a much happier person now and a much fuller person, too. She has found what is inside her and has discovered what was missing from her life.

DESTINY AND FATE

From the moment our souls are conceived our lives are fated and will follow a predetermined course. The major events in our lives, such as our births, marriages, separations and ultimately our deaths, are determined by a divine force.

However, it is not just these major events that are set down on our map of life. At our conception it is also determined who will be our soul mate. Before we are even born into this world another soul is paired with our own. From the earliest age of all we are all spiritually linked to another person, another soul. So when you meet a couple who are described as fated to be together, the fact is that they were.

I know that the idea of fate is alarming to some people because they do not like the idea of not having free will. People do not like to think of themselves as a puppet playing out a role that has already been determined by a higher force. The individual likes to believe that they have the power to shape their own destiny, that they have free will.

What is the point of trying to make a difference to our lives when they are already fated? There will, after all, be no decisions to make, no chances to take, nothing we could do to alter the course of our or anyone else's life. We might as well just resign ourselves to the fact that we cannot change our destinies. We might as well just sit back and wait for it all to happen and then die, for the course of life is inevitable, they argue.

As someone who holds both Spiritualist and Romany beliefs, I do believe that parts of our lives are destined. I believe that we all were destined to exist, for example, that some of us are destined to have children, that some of us are destined to help many people, that some of us are destined to die early. I believe that some things in life happen for a reason. You lose your job, for example, because you were destined to do something much greater with your life. You may be destined to do something that will benefit a great many people in the future. You may have been destined to die young because in your death a great many people would live on.

I believe these landmarks are mapped out before we are born but I would like to stress that they might not be achieved. A woman who is destined to reach a grand old age may still go before her time because she is killed in a road accident. We all have a destiny, but it is mostly up to us to make it happen, and to be aware of what is going on around us as destiny can'y always be taken for granted.

I like to think of life as a journey. Your birth signifies the start of that journey, and your death is your arrival at your ultimate destination. The journey that you are going to take has already been mapped out for you. Along the way you come across some landmarks. Some of these you will recognize, others you won't. Now whatever happens along the way you will arrive at your eventual destination, but there are many routes you can take to get there. One route may take you to a secure job, the other to a life in another country, and so on.

In my experience only the major events in one's life are predestined. While we are all destined to do certain things and encounter various souls along the way, not every aspect of our lives is *fated*. Predestination serves only as a blueprint for significant events. As I have said, there are many different routes we can take on that journey and it is up to the individual to choose the way. We still have choice, reason and the ability to make our own decisions. Sometimes the path you take may not be the best one. We may choose a longer route or get lost along the way; sometimes the path will be easy. But the journey we take, the path we follow, the routes we choose are up to us.

But the one thing, which I believe is absolutely determined before we are born, is the identity of our soul mate. Each and every one of us is given a special person with whom we are supposed to be either in this life or in the afterlife. For each soul is another perfectly matched soul, a soul with whom we are meant to be.

The reason why we feel such an affinity with our soul mate is that a higher, spiritual force – the spirit world – has sent you someone with whom you are spiritually compatible. You and your soul mate will always be bound together because your souls are alike. Your soul mate is special to you because they have been divinely chosen for you. It is as though someone who really knows and understands you, even better than you do yourself, has hand-picked this individual for you. And it is this link that gives you that great sense of belonging.

However, just because we are all destined to have a soul mate and that their identity has been predetermined, this does not mean we can sit back and wait for a tall dark stranger to come and knock on our door one afternoon. I am afraid that there are no guarantees that you will even find them in this life – this is something I will go into in Chapter Three. You have to make life work for you. We all make our destinies to an extent. We are on our journey, we cannot afford to sit down by the side of the road, instead we must keep finding the different paths to take. Your soul mate may be at the end of a short and obvious route, but you may also not meet them till the end of your journey. For fate to take its course you must live your life – to the full.

THE FUTURE

To an extent we are all intrigued to know what lies ahead for us, which is why, in my experience, so many reasonable and rational people resort to slightly more alternative practices in order to find out what their future is. It is only because our lives are, to some extent, fated, that a medium is able to tell a person what lies ahead for them in the future. The gift of prophesying or predicting future events is what is known as futurizing.

It is important to realize that when a medium speaks to you about the future it is not the medium who is telling you what the future holds for you but your spirit guides. A medium is not a prophet; they cannot look into the future. What they do is act as a channel between the spirit world and this world. They hear the voices and messages from a world that most people cannot communicate with. Mediums are able to interpret signs and symbols but without the help of the spirit world they are unable to tell you anything at all.

The act of prophecy lies with your spiritual guides, those spirits who watch over and guide your life. We all have a spirit guide, they are usually a person with whom we have some kind of connection who has passed away and it is their duty to act as our guardian angels. When you have a reading from a medium these spirits come forward and tell the mediums things about your past present and your future. The medium, as the word suggests, mediates between you and your spirit guide, communicating these messages to you. So if I were to say to you during a reading that you will meet your soul mate, he will be called Tony, he drives a blue car and you will meet through your work, these are not my predictions but the prophecies of your spirit guides. No human being, no matter how insightful or gifted, is able to know this information. As mortals we do not have access to this information, which is why I like to be known as a medium as opposed to a fortune teller.

Because the main events of our lives and the identity of our soul mate is predestined the spirit guides are aware of what our future is. But because they also visit us during the day they also know what is going on in our lives. They know what is worrying us, what we are fearful of, who is upsetting us, and because they can visit other people in our lives too, they know what is going to happen. This way they are able through a medium to advise us and tell us who to avoid, where not to go and so forth.

Because your spirit guides love you and have been appointed to care for you they will warn you off people. They will know, for example, that the man you are seeing is not for you because they have seen him with other women. They might know that the woman you are married to is using you and taking advantage of your generosity. They can do this because they have been with them when you are not around. Spirit guides are there to protect you.

Some people, particularly those who have been very

unhappy, ask me why, if their spirit guides love them so much, have they suffered so much? Surely, if their mother, who has passed away, could see them and still cared for them she would find them a soul mate? This is not, I am afraid, how it works. The fact is that whilst spirits can steer you in the right direction and help you, they cannot change or interfere with what is ultimately your destiny. It is your life and you must live it. A medium can give you an idea of what can happen to you in your life but it is up to you to make it happen.

SELF AND SOUL

To help destiny along its course, you must first be prepared to help yourself. You will only ever meet your soul mate when you are at one with your soul. This is because it is at this moment you are at your most attractive, confident and, most important of all, yourself. Your soul mate will see you always for exactly what you are and who you are. Unlike other relationships that you might have had, you will not have to pretend to your soul mate that you are someone else. So begin with being true to yourself. It is only when you are in this state that your soul mate will recognize you for who you really are.

The most important thing of all is to be at one with yourself and this means trying to understand who you are in the first place. You must learn to be comfortable with yourself before you expect others to be. You must learn to acknowledge what you want and don't want from life. I am not saying we should necessarily start chanting 'I love myself' around the house or anything silly like that. Nor do I suggest that you become self-obsessed. But if we are to move forward in love we need to discover ourselves and look into our souls. This is never easy. None of us is perfect and we may be hiding things from ourselves. But once you have opened your soul you may find what you are really looking for in life.

TWO

Recognizing Your Soul Mate

Your soul mate is not necessarily the type of person you might imagine them to be. When we are young we picture ourselves living for ever with some ideal man or woman. They are probably extremely attractive, successful and well off. But as we get older and more experienced our vision of our perfect partner changes. This is not because we don't want to be with an attractive, wealthy and successful person when we grow up! It is because we recognize our partner will have other attributes if they are to be our soul mate. Our notions of what might be 'perfect' develop as we mature. Because we do not know who we are when we are very young, we do not know what we really want or need. But as you grow older you get a better picture of what you want from life. And as that happens you begin to recognize the people with whom you want to share that life.

I cannot say to you here who your soul mate will be, but what I can do is show you what characteristics they will have so that you will be able to recognize them and look for them yourselves.

Your soul mate is a person with whom, from the outset, you have a special connection. He or she is someone to whom you are profoundly drawn. On first meeting your soul mate you will find that you instantly click, that there is a rapport. You feel that no one else in the room matters. They are someone with whom you have chemistry. You seem to spark off each other. So intrigued are you by them, you find yourself listening more than you want to talk.

The attraction you have for your soul mate may not be initially physical, in the sense that they might not be your usual type, if you have one, or your idea of your dream man or woman, yet there is something about them that is strangely alluring. It could be their mouth, the way that they laugh, or speak, the way that they hold themselves, the way that they move. Whatever it is, you find them bewitching.

A lot of people who have met their soul mate say that there was something in their eyes that first attracted them. I do not find this at all surprising. They say that the eyes are the windows of the soul and I find this to be true. The way a person uses their eyes can tell you a lot about them; whether they are caring or sensitive, whether they are confident or direct. The eyes rarely lie, which is why shifty people tend to look elsewhere when they are being dishonest. An honest person has no trouble looking another individual in the eye, for they have nothing to hide. Similarly, two people who find each other attractive will use their eyes to make contact with each other. A person who is devoted to another will tend to gaze adoringly at the object of their affection and a person who wants to know more about you will search your eyes with theirs.

Whatever our soul mate looks like to other people, in our eyes they are always beautiful. The physical attraction we feel to our soul mate is not about being a size ten, or having a straight nose or a full head of hair. For we see qualities in our soul mate that no one else can see. It is an attraction so strong that we cannot take our eyes off them. Other people may think our soul mate quite ordinary but to us they are compelling, fascinating and irresistible.

Your soul mate will be someone with whom you immediately feel comfortable. When you first meet, your heart may skip a beat at the mere mention of their name, you stomach may churn when you bump into them, but they should also, in time, be someone with whom you feel at one. With this person you should feel safe and secure. This is a very good indication as to whether or not you are with your soul mate, because your spirits would never put you together with anyone with whom you felt insecure.

A soul mate is not a person who would undermine you. They are not someone in whose company you feel threatened or small. Remember that you are given your soul mate so that you will be happy. Just as a parent would not want to see their child in a relationship with someone who belittles them, the spirit world has ensured that the person you are destined to be with will love, respect and care for you.

Your soul mate is not someone who would ever want you to change. They think the world of you as you are. He or she is a person with whom you should flourish, so it will be someone who is encouraging and positive. They want the best for you, they are on your side, and are always behind you. They might disagree with you from time to time, or give you advice that you don't think is right but ultimately their intention is for you to get the best out of life and to realize your potential.

He or she is a person who admires and respects you. A soul mate should never be patronizing to you or laugh at you. You should be able to talk to your soul mate about almost anything, however silly or trivial it might seem. They are someone with whom you can share your innermost thoughts and worries. A person with whom you should be able to share anything, they are your friend and your confidant. Your relationship with a soul mate should be honest. You should not be afraid of telling them anything because they love you *as you are*. They will never judge you, and whatever you do their opinion of you will not change.

You are always yourself when you are together. You never try to be anything more or someone different because you don't need to. You don't have to impress them to win them over. You never have to play games to make them like you. For you and your soul mate are bound spiritually, you reach each other's core, you understand each other's soul.

Your soul mate is someone you never tire of, they

are always of interest to you, and they never cease to surprise you. You should be able to have fun with them and laugh with them. A soul mate is a person you really enjoy being with. Whether you are just sitting at home together or out walking, it does not matter what you do together, because just being with each other is special in itself.

He or she may be someone who is the direct opposite of you. On the surface you may seem like chalk and cheese. Whilst you may be loud and forceful, they may be quiet and thoughtful. You may come from different backgrounds, different countries, be twenty years apart; none of that has any bearing on whether you are perfectly matched. People may ask, 'What do they see in each other?' You see more in each other than the naked eye could ever see. You see into each other's souls, which is why you have this deep, strong link. When your souls are bound in this way it does not matter what differences you have on the surface.

Between soul mates there is an unspoken language. The spiritual connection between you both is so deep that you seem to be able to communicate without even speaking to each other. You are happy to lie in silence together. You feel sometimes that there is no need to talk because you feel that you know what they are thinking anyway. You feel so close to them that sometimes you think you could almost read their mind. You know when they are worried, in pain, or sad just by looking at them. It is as though there exists some kind of telepathy between you. Often you think the same things at the same times. You are able to finish each other's sentences. 'How did you know I was going to say that?' they ask. You aren't even sure yourself. It just happens. It is as though there is a secret language between you. People who are soul mates may be very different on the outside but their souls are very alike, which is why they are able to communicate and understand each other in this way. Soul mates are kindred spirits.

Many people who have found their soul mate experience in the first months of their relationship the feeling that life is suddenly worth living, the sky seems bluer, the grass greener, the world looks beautiful. This is because when you are with your soul mate your values change. Your outlook on life alters because at that moment you become more spiritual. The simple pleasures in life become the greatest pleasures in life and this is because you feel fulfilled. What was missing in your life before, that thing you were searching for, has been found. When we fall in love suddenly the things we thought were important, such as our careers, our popularity, our aspirations, fade away. We realize that these things will never bring us as much happiness as the relationship we have with our soul mate.

Because of this sense of fulfilment, however independent you are as a person, you will find that you cannot bear to be separated from your soul mate. When you are alone and in another environment you find yourself wishing that they could be there to share it with you. You think about them without meaning to throughout the day. When you hear their name mentioned it makes you smile. They are someone you want to touch, to hold, and to talk to. They are someone you just want to be with. Someone you want to spend your life with.

People often ask me how they will know whether they have found their soul mate. They want to know what characteristics their soul mate will have and how they will be able to distinguish their soul mate from other people. They worry that they might not be able to recognize them when they do eventually meet.

I always say to people when they ask me this, you *will* know, it is as simple as that. It will be instinctive. You will feel it inside you, like a gut reaction. Those who have already met their soul mate say that it is impossible not to know when you do find them for it just feels so right. They say that it is different from any feeling that they have ever had for anyone in the past.

People say that it is like finding their other half, in that until they met their soul mate they were aware that was something lacking in their life. When you meet your soul mate that gap is instantly filled. People talk about feeling fulfilled and whole. That until they met their soul mate they felt like they were only half-alive. One expression I hear time and time again from those who are looking for love is, 'there is something missing in my life'. Until we find our soul mates there is indeed something missing, because we are all, of course, destined to share our lives with another soul.

The attraction we feel for our soul mate is not only instinctive but it is also instant. It may not be love at first sight in the traditional sense. You may not feel that this is the person with whom you want to spend the rest of your life when you first meet them, but there is definitely something there. Something you may not be able to put your finger on even, but nevertheless it is a strong feeling of attraction.

People feel very drawn to their soul mate when they first meet them. They may not fancy them, they may not feel passionate about them, they may not even like them, but they are deeply affected by them. It is as though they have got into the very core of your being. The attraction you feel towards your soul mate is so intense and strong, it is as though they are pulling you into some magnetic field. However hard you try you cannot escape from this feeling, you cannot resist them. The more you get to know them, the more intense this attraction becomes. Nothing can keep you apart.

It is a totally different sensation to infatuation or pure physical attraction. It is a feeling from within. Your feelings may surprise you. You may even ask yourself, 'Why am I attracted to them?' You may not be able to explain your feelings but you cannot deny them either.

One of the first signs of falling in love with a person is being unable to get them out of your mind. Once your soul mate has 'got to you' in this way, whether you are out with friends, getting on with your job, or shopping, your mind keeps going back to this person again and again. No matter how hard you try to concentrate on other things in your life you cannot help yourself thinking about them.

Similarly, when you are separated, not a day can pass without you thinking of them. You find yourself wondering what they are doing, what they are thinking, whether they are thinking of you, too. If you are soul mates you can guarantee that they will be.

It is quite normal when you meet your soul mate to feel as though you have known them all your life, even though you may have known them for no longer than half an hour! This is because you have this spiritual bond, because you are kindred spirits. You see, however different you are on the outside, deep down you are compatible and similar.

Before you have known them for very long you already know what they like and dislike, what they care about, what is important to them. It is more that just having something in common. It is more than just coincidence. For somewhere deep inside you know them already. It is as though you have met in another life, and in many ways, because of your spiritual connection, you have. When you enter their home for the first time you may experience a sense of déjà vu. It is as though you have seen their house in a dream.

When Marion first met her soul mate John she felt

that she already knew so much about him, even before they had got to know each other properly. She tells her story here in her own words:

MARION

I met John through a friend. We were out having a drink one night in our local pub when he came up to the table and said hello to Patricia. She hadn't seen him for a while so he stayed for a drink, and I instantly liked him. He was very friendly and quite self-assured. I was having an outdoor party the following Saturday. It was a very casual thing, just a few drinks and food in my garden over the Bank Holiday weekend. I asked John if he wanted to come with Patricia. He said he would love to.

I had decided that I was going to make paella for the party but when I went to the fishmonger that morning something in my head kept telling me to make something different for John. I kept thinking, 'You must get something else because he gets sick when he eats mussels.' It was very strange because John and I had only met once. He had stayed in the pub with us for no longer than twenty minutes and there was no talk of food, allergies or anything like that. In fact, we had only talked about Patricia's ex while he was there! I never spoke to Patricia about John, either. I knew nothing about him, yet I was certain of this one thing.

That night John came to the party and sure

enough he didn't touch the paella. Instead, he went for the chicken salad I had also made. 'I hope you don't think me rude,' he said, as I passed him a knife and fork, 'It looks great, but I just can't eat mussels, even though I love them. I had bad food poisoning after eating them once so I've never touched them since.'

I don't know how I knew that John couldn't eat mussels. It's not as though you can tell something like this just from looking at someone. It may seem trivial to some people, or that it was just a coincidence, but to me it felt very significant.

It wasn't the only thing like this that happened either. It was as though I had a sixth sense about John. I felt as though, for some reason, I already knew this man, that there was a part of me that understood him. And I think I must have because we have been together now for over four years.

Some people I have come across not only think they know things about their soul mate they actually feel that they have met them before, even though they haven't. Some people have said to me that they have dreamt about their soul mate before they have actually met them. This isn't a case of dreaming or fantasizing about your ideal and then meeting someone who fits that mould. In these dreams people have said they have seen a specific person who they then went on to meet.

Carla said that when she met her soul mate Tom she already knew what he looked like. They met at a work function; they had never seen each other before; they had not known of each other before their initial meeting; they knew no one in common.

CARLA

It was such a shock because when he walked into the room I instantly recognized him. I was about to go and say hello but I realized that we had never met. We couldn't have done anyway, because it was his first time in the country.

I realized that I had seen him the night before, not in the flesh but in an extremely vivid dream. He was wearing exactly the same blue cord jacket, navy shirt and chino trousers. He was carrying a book in one hand and a green scarf in the other, just as he had in the dream. I know that I wasn't imagining my dream, because that morning I had told my flatmate about it because it was so vivid.

The reason why this happens is that our spirit guides like to help fate along its way. They might show you an image of your soul mate in your dreams, or tell you things about them, because they want you to recognize your soul mate. They are helping love take its course, nudging you in the right direction. For people who really do believe that they have known their soul mate before it is possible that you have met in another life. It could be that you have lived a previous life, in which case you will have been with your soul mate before. But for the majority of us the fact that we have been paired as souls before our births creates this feeling of knowing and belonging. The link that we have as individuals makes us feel that we are at one when we do eventually meet and get together.

Because the bond we have with our soul mate is so strong, because we feel we know them already and because of the mutual understanding we have for each other relationships between soul mates can happen almost overnight. The getting to know you process is much shorter than it would be in any other relationship because there is so much between you already.

The connection that you are making is a very spiritual one so the more practical questions we would normally ask a person, such as where did you go to school, where are you from and so forth, lose their significance. You have already found your common ground. There are so many things that make you click, so many different levels on which you relate that the things you would normally discuss with a prospective lover seem irrelevant to your situation. With your soul mate you don't have to search for things in common because they already exist. You are not basing your relationship on mutual friends, common pursuits or shared experiences because you do not need to. You feel you belong with them, and that is enough.

I am never surprised when soul mates have whirlwind relationships. When you meet your soul mate there is nothing wrong with taking things quickly. Some people may think you are rushing into it, but when you know that you have found your soul mate then there is no need to take your time. If they *are* your soul mate there is no need to feel either cautious or hesitant. The courtship that is so necessary in any other affair is not essential here. If you feel that this person really is the one and only, you can rest assured that then you are doing the right thing by being with them.

I always say that you meet your soul mate in strange circumstances or places. I know people who have spent their lives accepting invitations to parties, attending dinners and going out at night in the hope of meeting their dream man or woman, only to bump into them at the bus stop, at the supermarket checkout or halfway up a mountain. I know people who have met their soul mate by walking into them, literally. One woman I know met hers when she crashed her car into his. Another met hers through her ex-husband's new girlfriend and one couple I know met on a car ferry.

I am not suggesting that you will only find your soul mate if you hang out in unglamorous locations or serially try to write off your car! The point I am trying to make is that we meet our soul mate when we least expect it. You and your soul mate are destined to find each other when you do; you cannot get up one day and decide, 'This is it, today's the day.' It just doesn't work like that.

You may be very keen to find a mate and so you go to as many parties and events as you can. You may meet a lot of very eligible people and have a great deal of fun.

But it may just be that the time simply isn't right to find your soul mate – or the time may be right but the place isn't.

Our spirit guides want us to have fulfilling and happy lives and so they will go out of their way to help us find true love. This is why we tend to meet our soul mates in very strange places. They are so desperate for us to find the person who they already know is our soul mate, they push us to go to places that we had no intention of ever visiting, sometimes as a sign that something out of the ordinary is at work.

You might be walking to the office one morning, for example. That day, for the first time in two years you change your route. You don't know why you are doing it, it may even make you late for work, but you do it all the same. It is as if you are on autopilot, as though you are not in control of what you are doing, where you are going, as though you are being guided by another force. And in a way you are. A spirit has whispered in your 'inner' ear, changing your route, making you alter your plans.

You walk down the road, and see a bus coming, you take it. On this bus you start talking to the man next to you. He is going to tell you where to get off. This man turns out to be your soul mate. Had you not taken the bus or changed your route you would not have met then. Later on when you are a couple you will say, 'What if I hadn't taken the bus that day, we would never have met!' 'It was fate,' your soul mate will say. And it was. But had you not taken that bus that day you would have met at another time. As I said in Chapter One, much of our life is mapped out – we will meet our soul mate one day because we were destined to do so. However, there are many different paths we can take to get to that destination. And had you not met your soul mate that particular day, your spirit guides would have ensured that you did at some other point.

When it comes to love and finding your soul mate there are no such things as coincidences. Our meetings may seem to be chance encounters but in fact they have been carefully choreographed by our spirit guides.

Although we are all destined to be with our soul mates, although we may be searching for 'the one', you should realize that you may not meet them for many years. Soul mates do not necessarily turn up when we want them to, in our twenties or thirties for example. You may have to wait your whole lifetime. I know of people who met their soul mate when they were in their late eighties.

We may be ready to meet our soul mate and want it very badly but they may not be ready to be with us. We may recognize our soul mate when we meet them, but if the time is not right for us to be together, it won't happen then. It is all about synchronicity. Sometimes our timing is not quite right. We may have met but we are not yet destined to be together. In cases like these you just have to be patient.

Tara was seeing a number of men last summer. She

had lots of fun but she had yet to meet the one and only. But towards September she met a man whom she really liked and fell for. Their rapport was instant, but then things went downhill. The relationship she had hoped for fizzled out.

TARA

I had dated quite a few men last year. They were all great in their own way, attractive and fun, but I found that there was always something missing in these relationships. My friends thought I was being fussy. The men I was seeing were all eligible. They were clever, good-looking and fun to be with. I just didn't seem to click with any of them. I thought that there might be something wrong with me.

I was about to resign myself to the fact that I might never find anyone really special when at the end of the summer I fell in love. I was at a party when I met Tony. I can't say that it was a very romantic first meeting. I had just bumped into someone and they had knocked red wine all over my trousers. I was about to fly off the handle, I hadn't been having a very good day, when this very sweet man rushed over to me with a cloth and some salt. 'Try this,' he said laughing. 'I can't believe that someone else is as clumsy as I am.' We were laughing and from that moment we got on really well.

We started seeing each other a lot. I liked him because he was just so easy to get on with. I began thinking, 'This is it.' Which was funny really, as he wasn't my type at all. He wasn't conventionally good-looking but I found him very attractive. I couldn't put my finger on what it was about him, there was just something so wonderful. We went out a lot and spent most of our free time together. We spoke for hours on the telephone at night talking about nothing. I had never had a relationship with anyone like this, not even my best friend.

And then just as quickly as it began, it ended. Out of the blue he just seemed to back off. He didn't call and when I telephoned him he was always on the way out of the door. I couldn't think what I had done wrong. I kept thinking that I must have said something that had offended him. It was all so sudden.

I was very upset. I couldn't stop thinking about him. My friends were very unsympathetic. They couldn't see what I saw in him and kept telling me things like, 'There are plenty more fish in the sea,' which didn't help. And I began to feel that maybe I wanted Tony so much because I could not have him.

A month later I spoke to Rita. When I rang for my appointment she only knew my Christian name and my star sign. Rita said that she had my mother in spirit. She told me she had passed away with cancer, which she had. She told me a lot of very personal things that would mean nothing to anyone else but meant a lot to me.

Because of the information she gave me I knew

she had to be for real, so when she started talking about my future I had faith in what she was saying. Rita said to me that I would get married within a year and that I would have two children. She knew I had been dating a lot, and named a couple of people I had been seeing. 'He's not right for you, oh no,' she would say as a name came up. Then she said, 'Your soul mate has the initial "A".' I was disappointed. I thought she would say that it was Tony but she kept saying 'A'. She told me that I knew him already. I kept thinking, 'I hope she doesn't mean Adrian,' who was a man who had taken me out that summer. We carried on with the reading when she said out of the blue, 'Anthony! You know an Anthony, don't you?' I couldn't think what she was talking about. 'You do, you like him very much but you haven't seen him for a while.' That's when I realized. She was talking about Tony.

Rita told me that I had to be patient. 'Stop worrying yourself,' she said. 'Just because you are ready for this relationship does not mean that he is, he has things to sort out before he can be with you.' Rita said that Tony had come out of a very long affair and that he had been badly bruised by the break-up. 'He doesn't love her any more, but he's scared of being hurt again,' she said.

Rita told me that my mother was saying that he would call me. She said that he thought about me a lot. She said that he needed to know that I was serious about him but in time things would work out for us.

> *Tony did call about a month later. We went for coffee and he told me that he had been badly hurt by an unfaithful girlfriend. We have taken it very slowly since then, day by day. But I know that in time things will work out for both of us.*

Tara and Tony were obviously soul mates and I think that they both must have recognized this from the moment they met. But just because we meet our soul mate it does not follow we are suddenly able or ready to begin a deep and meaningful relationship with them overnight. We may be destined to be together, but not just yet.

Similarly, there are many soul mates who already know each other but haven't realized it yet because the time isn't right. It may be because you are too young, or you are with someone else. But don't worry because they will come back into your life.

When soul mates meet when they are very young, they may not realize that they are destined for each other. They are merely friends. They may have grown up and been to school together and then drifted apart as their lives took course. It could be the case that when young they did not even like each other. It is only as they mature that they begin to appreciate each other. But for those who have been friends in youth when they meet again in adulthood it is as though not a day has passed.

When Mary met her soul mate John she had been

married for ten years to another man. I knew in her readings that her husband was making her unhappy and I sensed that there was someone that Mary had known many, many years ago who was going to come back into her life. Mary refused to believe me. She admitted that she was unhappy in her marriage and that she felt unfulfilled but she felt loyal to her husband. I told her I knew she was going to find her soul mate but that she must go home. I said that he was a 'J', and I saw him there in a white coat. But Mary was not having any of it.

It was fate that led Mary to John. One night a couple of years ago Mary got a telephone call from someone in the town where she grew up. Mary had not been there in years, not since her mother had passed away when Mary was in her early twenties. The call came from an old lady who had lived in Mary's street who wanted her to know that Dawn was very ill. Dawn had been like a grandmother to Mary when she was growing up. Whenever her mother was at work, or out at night, Dawn would come and look after Mary. She did not have any family of her own so she used to like to spoil Mary. So when Mary heard that she was ill she knew that it was her turn to look after her.

When Mary arrived at Dawn's that evening a neighbour told her that Dawn's usual doctor would not be in that week because he was on holiday. Instead the locum would be visiting later. The neighbour said she did not know him but he sounded very charming on the telephone. 'He's called Dr Reynolds,' the neighbour said. The name meant nothing to Mary. She did not know then that this was the man I had been talking about in her reading. Dr Reynolds, John Reynolds, had been at Mary's school. He was a couple of years older than she was, and Mary had been very taken with him. But when Mary went to London they lost touch.

It must have been twenty years since they had last seen each other but when John walked through the door of Dawn's house they recognized each other instantly. 'Mary!' he said when he saw her. 'You are as pretty as ever, you haven't changed a bit!' Throughout that week John dropped round to the house more and more frequently. They spent hours catching up and reminiscing. On their last evening together as John was leaving the house he turned to her and said, 'I was very sad when you left here, Mary, it broke my heart. I was always very keen on you, you must have known that. I only wish you'd stayed here with me.'

At the end of the week Mary had to return to London. A month later her husband left. Mary was not upset, she was relieved. She was glad that he had realized that they could no longer go on like that. There was nothing keeping her from John any longer and so Mary took a train up north to see her 'J', the man in the white coat.

The problem that many people suffer from in relationships is that they think they are in love when they aren't. Sometimes we want love so much that we convince ourselves that we are truly in love with a person. We imagine that the person who we are seeing is right for us. We attribute qualities to them they do not have. We put them on a pedestal, believe that they are perfect and spend the rest of the relationship convincing our friends, families and ourselves that this is the case.

But remember you cannot make someone your soul mate if they are not. Soul mates aren't things we can create. We cannot decide that the person we like at the moment is going to be our soul mate. They either are your soul mate, or they aren't! You cannot force it. If you are with someone you like, and who likes you, but together you lack the chemistry I have described in this chapter, then my advice is move on and wait. That person is not right for you. You will find true love eventually, and when it does come your way, it will have been worth waiting for.

When we fall for people, when we feel passionate about them or are infatuated by them, we may feel that we have found our soul mate. The emotions we go through at the beginning of any affair can be very similar to those we feel for our soul mate when we first meet them. You may be giddy, joyful and ecstatic. You may feel as though you have a bond, that you never wish to be parted from them. In the first stages of a love affair you may feel all these things but the real test is whether they last or not. You see, the love between soul mates is always like this. It doesn't fade or tire. You never get bored of your soul mate or wish they were something that they are not.

A lot of young people I meet become very concerned with finding their soul mate, because they are keen to get married. Marriage is a great thing if it works out. And it is quite possible to have a perfectly happy and satisfactory marriage with someone who is not your soul mate but with whom there is mutual love and respect. However, you have more chance of having a successful and happy marriage if you wait for your soul mate. I would advise anyone in this position to hang back. Getting married is not the important thing. It is far better to wait for the right man or woman than to rush ahead and marry the wrong person just for the sake of it.

You can usually tell whether you have met your soul mate or not by asking yourself a few honest questions and by looking critically at the situation in hand.

- If you have a choice between two men, for example, and cannot seem to make up your mind, then you have not found your soul mate.
- If you are at all hesitant, then you are not with your soul mate.
- Are you with a person because there is no one else in your life, because you want to be married, or just because you have been seeing each other for a long time?
- Are you with someone because they offer you security and a lifestyle you would not have on your own?
- Are you with them because you cannot bear to be on your own?

If the answer to any of these last three questions is yes then you have not found your soul mate yet. But on the other hand, if after years of being together you wake up with them and you are happy and still laughing, if you can do simple things together and still be in love, if you feel like your life would end if you were ever parted, then you are with the right person.

THREE

Finding the One, Finding Yourself

Finding your soul mate goes hand in hand with finding out who you really are as a person. Sometimes we make mistakes in relationships because we are not paying close enough attention to what we want from life and who we want to be with.

To find the right person to share your life with you have to be in touch with your identity. Often we choose people in life who are wrong for us and this is because we are not really sure what we are looking for. We think we want to be with someone because they are, for example, fun and because they always seem to be having a good time. But after a while the novelty of this can wear off and we find that there is nothing more to the person we have chosen to be with. Suddenly we find ourselves not only wanting but also needing more. We discover we have not got what we need and so the relationship breaks down, and we are left wondering whether we will ever find the right person.

Of course, the right person has already been 'found' for you. Your soul mate was matched with you before you were even born. You are destined to be together and fate, hopefully, will take you to them within your lifetime. However, there are things we can do to help destiny along its way. We want to be prepared for the time when we do find our soul mate and we want to know that when they do walk into our lives we will recognize that they are 'the one'. Furthermore, just because our lives are predestined, this does not mean that we should sit back and wait for someone to walk into our lives and find us.

Being true to yourself is the first and most important step you can take when you are searching for true love and everlasting happiness. If you are honest about how you feel about yourself, the rest will follow. When you understand who you are you will begin to know what you want from people, from your career and from your life. By learning to love yourself you will discover the kind of love you are searching for.

YOUR SELF

Looking deep within can help us understand who we are. It is not an easy process because as humans we tend to hide things even from ourselves. We all have as individuals many qualities. We may be kind, generous, compassionate, sensitive, imaginative, loving. We all have something to offer. But we also have many things within our character that make our lives more difficult. Often the good comes with the bad. By this I mean that your strongest points are at times also your weakest.

Honesty is a quality that springs to mind. Honesty is

widely regarded as a virtue and people admire a person who is always honest, a person who will always tell the truth, a person who speaks from the heart. We would all like to be honest and to be around honest people. And yet honesty can also cause difficulties when you are involved in a relationship, with a soul mate, a member of your family or even a friend. Honesty can often offend other people. Sometimes we speak our mind when it is better, or perhaps more diplomatic, to be silent. Sometimes our honesty can lead to difficulties within a relationship.

Similarly, a sensitive person who is always in tune with the feelings of others can be weakened by this characteristic. They may find at times that their sensitivity leads them to being too eager to please, they tread around an issue not wanting to make anyone feel unhappy so they end up in situations that have, perhaps, compromised their position or integrity. A person who is strong may help others and lead them in the right direction but at the same time they may be in danger of undermining another person.

Getting to know yourself before you get to know another person can be useful because you learn to understand that balance is key to making a relationship work. Understanding that your strengths may also be your weaknesses will help you to live within a relationship.

It should also make you realize not only what you want from another individual but also what you need. A person who is strong by nature may think, for example, that they would be attracted to another strong person. But often I find that this is a misconception. Do we really want to be with a person we are going to be challenged with day in day out, or do we want someone who is going to counterbalance our personality?

Not knowing who we are can lead to very serious problems in our lives and often results in us ending up with the wrong person. People who have found their soul mate often tell me that before they found them there was a certain type they went for. They were convinced they liked people who looked a certain way, for example. They thought they wanted to be with a person who shared all their interests and friends. They chose to be with people who were as ambitious as they were. They saw this as being indicative of wanting the same things out of life.

The problem with this way of thinking is that I am not sure that people do really know what they want out of life. A man who says he likes blondes who like football and adventure holidays is a man who *does not* know what he wants from life. Long-lasting happiness in life is not just about hair colour, hobbies and holidays. Life-long happiness comes from the ability to be at peace with your soul mate and yourself. It is about finding something that is deeper and more profound together. Certainly finding a soul mate who has the same interests or a mate who you are sexually attracted to helps. But you have to ask yourself whether you will be happy with that person in fifty years time. When the blonde turns to grey, when you've grown out of football and are too old for white-water rafting, what then?

The reason why we make so many mistakes in love is that we do not know what we are really after. Often we think we like a person because we think we know what we want. But until you really know yourself you will never really understand what you want and so you will carry on making the same mistakes time and time again.

Getting to know yourself, and being in touch with your identity can make your life much easier. If you care about yourself and are at peace with yourself you will gain inner strength. Sometimes a little introspection is not such a bad thing. When you learn what you are like spiritually you will not only find peace but also confidence.

Many people think that because they are on their own it is a sign to everyone else that no one wants them. Being single should be a choice that you make. Even if you have been deserted by a lover or abandoned in a marriage you must remember that this may have been best for you. You do not *need* to have someone. It is wonderful if you do, but you should never think that you are less of a person for being on your own.

When someone has been through a relationship that has not worked out, or with a person to whom they were not suited, it can affect their confidence badly. They can end up thinking very little of themselves because they imagine that they are not good enough, not right for someone else. People who have been rejected often suffer terribly from low self-esteem. You think that there must be something wrong with you, instead of thinking, 'Why didn't *this* work out?' There is likely nothing wrong with either of you individually, you just weren't right *together*. The fact that your last relationship may have ended may be sad, you may feel very hurt and isolated, but in time those wounds can heal, and the pain of those feelings you are experiencing can be forgotten.

The human psyche is actually more resilient that we think. I cannot count the amount of times I have had people sitting in my reading room crying about a past lover. 'I'll never get over it. There will never be anyone else. I will never fall in love again!' they say. I smile to myself. You *will* get over it, you *will* feel better, and in time you will wonder what on earth you ever saw in that person. You don't have to be psychic to see this, but sometimes it does help – because often as these people sit in front of me sobbing into their hankies a voice in my 'inner' ear is telling me that they are about to meet their soul mate.

The first thing you can do to make things better is to start looking forward. When something has failed it is easy to sit there staring out of the window wondering what might have been, reminiscing over the good times, plotting how you might win your lover back, feeling sorry for yourself. You have to stop that and think about your future. Think about the good things in your life, about why other people find you special. Looking inside yourself, being in touch with your spiritual nature, your soul, you will slowly begin to realize what you *really* want from your life. And then I think you will find that it is not the lost relationship you are mourning.

The next step is to get back into your life, the life you had before you met that person. Surrounding yourself with old friends and members of your family can be very healing. They will remind you about what you have to offer as an individual and that will give you more confidence. When we are feeling good about ourselves we can take charge of our lives and we have a greater hold on our destiny. The second step is to realize that it is your life and you must live it. I have said that our lives are subject to predestination but only aspects of it. You are in control of your day-to-day life. If you want to make your dreams a reality you can. Never put your life on hold. Even if I were to tell you who your soul mate is, don't expect them to come knocking on your door. You have to go out there and be ready to find them, to recognize them.

You must believe in yourself, not wait for someone to believe in you. You should not rely on others to love you and give you confidence when you have no faith in yourself.

When Pippa came to see me she was extremely low. She felt that there was no meaning to her life. At the age of thirty-six she had had a string of affairs, but none of them had ever amounted to anything. She was very talented, good at her job, but it no longer gave her the fulfilment she needed. Pippa had begun to feel that she had wasted too much time concentrating on her career and not enough on her personal relationships.

During our reading Pippa's mother came to me. She told me that her name was Daphne and that she had passed away after a long battle with cancer. She told me that Pippa had a new flat and that it was by the sea. She visits her there regularly and knew that she had just bought some new furniture.

Daphne told me to tell Pippa that she was proud of her daughter and that she was glad that she had so many loving friends. Daphne said that Pippa should be strong because great things were about to happen. She was going to be offered a new job in the coming months and she said that Pippa should take it because it was going to give her the challenge she needed at this stage of her life. When Pippa heard me say that her mother had good news for her I think she was disappointed to hear that it was about a new job. What she wanted was not a new job but a new relationship.

But Daphne said that Pippa should not see her career as a waste because it would be *through* this new job that Pippa would meet her soul mate. She was saying that a man would come to her through her work and that it would be love at first sight. He would be single, smartly dressed and love boats she said. This man would not think of her as a failure because she had not had a steady relationship; instead, he would admire her for her work and love her for herself.

She said that she knew that Pippa was worried about

spending her life on her own and that would not happen. If Pippa stopped worrying she would have a better chance of finding love. Her mother then showed me an image of two people with a child on a boat. She was desperate for me to tell her daughter that she would be happy in the future.

In order to 'find' our soul mates we need to stop feeling so negative about who we are. Often the way we imagine ourselves is not actually who we are or how others see us.

When you feel fulfilled as a person you may not even feel that you need or want to have a soul mate. For so many people it is just as they are getting themselves together that they meet someone. Again, this is not coincidence, this is because they are at their most attractive and thus attracting the right kind of person.

Although our lives are predestined, although we all have a soul mate ear-marked for us at conception, this does not mean we can afford to sit back and wait for a tall, dark, handsome stranger to walk through our door. We may be fated to meet our soul mate, but it may well be that we will not meet them in this life. Destiny only works if we live out our lives.

I once came across a girl who had been told by a Tarot card reader that she would have a relationship with a dark, handsome stranger who would bring happiness into her life. The man she was told in the reading would find her, so she should 'look no further'. Unfortunately, the girl took the reading somewhat too literally. She was so convinced that her soul mate would root her out and come to her that she stopped going out and seeing her friends. I think she was afraid she might miss him – that he might turn up while she was out. And so she stayed at home, waiting. Six months ago I received a letter from this girl asking whether I thought the clairvoyant she had seen had made a mistake. I am not a great believer in Tarot cards, but I think that the 'mistake' had been made by the girl – and not the clairvoyant.

When I read for the girl I saw that her soul mate would turn up in her life soon. I couldn't say whether he was this same dark stranger, but what I did know is that she wouldn't meet him if she locked herself away every night. Perhaps one day he would come knocking on her door, but there was no guarantee that he would. In the meantime she had to live her life and enjoy it.

When it comes to finding your soul mate you do have to make a bit of an effort. You cannot expect your spirit guides to do all the work for you. By living your life you create opportunities to meet your true love. Think of you and your soul mate's lives as parallel lines. You could go through your life living parallel existences, never having any contact with your soul mate until you die. What you want is for those lines, your lives, to intersect so that you can meet. By living your life to the full you can create those intersections. By choosing to do something one day that you might not do normally, by agreeing to go somewhere, you might end up at one of these predestined intersections and there they are.

I cannot begin to tell you how many people have found their soul mate by changing their plans at the last moment or by doing something out of character. They talk of it being a fluke, a chance encounter. I put it down to being in the right place at the right time. Destiny has created that time and that place – it is up to you to get yourself there. People say to me, 'Well how will I know?' The answer is you won't but if you follow your instincts, in your heart it will happen.

Unfortunately, we don't always find our soul mate as soon as we start looking. Finding your soul mate is rather like looking for your ideal house. It's rare that we walk into a property for the first time and think, 'This is it.' You have to keep looking. You may not know what you want when you first start looking but in the end you will have a very clear idea of what is right for you, and you keep looking until you come across it.

And just as you shouldn't buy a house because it is the first one you see, when it comes to relationships you should also take your time. You may take a property that isn't quite right temporarily, just as you might have a brief relationship, but never convince yourself that this is going to be your ideal home. If you haven't found your soul mate yet, don't despair. You *will* find them one day.

We search for a soul mate because we want to have

happy, fulfilling lives; you should want to find a soul mate because you want to be loved and give love. However, I think a mistake many people make is that they imagine that finding a soul mate is the answer to all their prayers and problems. If only that were true! A soul mate brings us love, and therefore happiness, but it doesn't mean they'll take away all the sorrows and pain in your life.

A person who is looking for someone to do this often won't find his or her soul mate in this life. What they want is someone who will give, give, and give. Your soul mate may be divinely chosen for you, they may be perfect in your eyes, but this does not make them divine themselves! They are human; they have their own needs as well. Be prepared to give in return. When you are experiencing unconditional love with your soul mate, this will happen naturally.

I do find that some people get quite impatient when it comes to searching for their soul mate. You must sit back and relax. What is the right time for you may not be the right time for your soul mate.

There is no point rushing into relationships believing the first person you feel anything for is 'the one'. Sometimes people are just too keen to find true love. They *try* to fall in love with the first person they meet, and this is when they make mistakes. My advice is to take your time. It is far better to wait and eventually find the right person than to force a relationship with someone who isn't for you, just for the sake of it. Attitudes may have changed to marriage and divorce, but rushing into something, convincing yourself you have found 'the one', is not something I recommend: more often than not you will find that you have made the wrong decision. When it comes to finding 'the one', there are, I am afraid to say, no short cuts.

When I met Jenny she was not having, as she put it, much luck with men. At twenty-four she had still not found *the* special one. She had broken up with her last boyfriend several years before, but she had not found anyone right for her. Jenny thought that maybe she was being too fussy. Was there a man of her dreams out there or was she, as her mother told her, being far too choosy?

Jenny had been dating a few boys whom she quite liked, but she was not sure when she came for a reading whether she should compromise and go out with them or sit back and wait for her Mr Right.

In her reading I picked up that she was a twin, which was very interesting to me. Her sister had found *her* soul mate, and was living abroad with him. I think that this had made Jenny more aware of her situation. She had effectively lost her sister, to whom she was incredibly close, when her sister moved away. Subconsciously, she felt that she had been replaced in her sister's affections by her sister's new boyfriend. She felt unbalanced because her sister was so happy and fulfilled in this relationship.

Jenny's spirit guide told me that her ex-boyfriend

Craig was trying to come back into her life, but the spirit guide also told me that he was not right for her. Jenny's dates were nice and well-meaning but none was the love of her life. But I did feel that Jenny's soul mate was already moving into her life. I felt that she knew him but not very well yet; however, in the next year this would develop. I knew that Jenny would not marry for two years but when she did it would be to her soul mate, and it would be worth the wait.

Just because your friends and family have found their soul mates, beware of rushing into a relationship just for the sake of not being on your own. It is neither fair on you nor the person with whom you compromise yourself. Love *will* come to you, but maybe not at the time that you would like. If it doesn't then it is for a reason. It is because the spirits planned for you to do something else first. You may have to meet someone else who will be important to your life, you may have to do something in your career, travel to a place. And though you do not realize this at the time, it could be that this other thing will actually lead you to your soul mate.

Splitting up from a relationship can be extremely hard and you may feel that you never want to go through another relationship again. But in my experience a break-up can often take us to the one we are destined to be with. It may be awful at the time and you may vow that there will never be anyone else. But usually it is this pain that takes us to the right place we need to be both mentally and literally.

Spirits, I am sorry to say, cannot stop bad things from happening to us. They can warn us about bad things coming our way that are not in our life map and so help us avoid them, but not if they are part of our destiny. However, while your mother in spirit cannot stop someone hurting you, she can make things better for you. As my grandmother used to say, 'Whatever harm comes to you, I'll reverse it.' Out of bad things come good things. A break-up can seem very harsh at the time but two years after you'll probably think, 'Thank goodness I'm rid of that person.' You will reach a stage when you cannot imagine what you saw in him or her, how you put up with their personality, and you will be grateful it happened because it means that you are now free to meet your soul mate. This is certainly true of Peter. He thought that when his relationship with Angela ended his life was over. In fact, it was only just the beginning. He tells his story here in his own words:

PETER

Five years ago I came back to London in high spirits from a year in America. Working out there had meant me being separated from my girlfriend Angela, and I also missed my family and friends. I loved America but realized that if Angela and I had a future I would have to come home. But when I got back, things had changed a great deal. My family were totally preoccupied by my sister's wedding plans, and my friends had become very involved with either work or girlfriends. Even seeing them for a drink in the pub was difficult. But the worst thing of all was seeing Angie. After so many months apart all the letters, the calls, counting the days till I would see her, she seemed distant and distracted. She didn't want me to touch her and she could not look me in the eye. Two days after I had got back she told me that it was no use trying to pretend any more. She said we had both changed and that while I had been away she had fallen for someone else with whom she wanted to settle down.

I felt like the rug had been pulled from under my feet. I could not believe what was happening. I spent so long idealizing my life in England, my future with her. I felt betrayed, hurt and angry all at once. So much ran through my head that I lost all reason and became very depressed. I said to her that I thought we should try to make a go of it all the same; we had been through too much to let it go. I wouldn't let it drop. A friend told me I needed some help; they gave me Rita's address and number. The idea of going to a psychic was alien to me: I did not believe in it at all, and I forgot about the suggestion. But one night I couldn't take it any more. I needed to talk to someone, whoever they were, because I knew I could not cope on my own.

Rita told me that my grandfather, Bert, was watching over me, and to my amazement she also began telling me about America, my sister's wedding and Angie. She even named the other man in her life. Rita told me that Angie was not my soul mate, and that I should go back to America. She said that this had all happened for a reason, which was to send me back to the place that for the moment was my real home. She said that eventually I would return to London, but for the moment I should go back to LA because although I would not meet my soul mate there, it would be by returning there that I would be led to this person.

To be honest, although I found what Rita said to be of comfort, I did not pay too much attention to it. I was not interested in future soul mates; I wanted Angie, and going back to LA was not that easy. I did not have a work permit any more, and there was no job to return to.

Three weeks later I was sitting in my parents' house when I got a phone call from my old boss in LA. He said, 'I'm sure you're all sorted back there, but I wanted to let you know that there's some more work for you back here if you're still interested.' He said that he would arrange my work permit and visa for me. That was that. There was nothing for me in London any more and I felt that somehow this was fated.

I returned to the US the following month to stay for six months and try to put the past behind me. In June I came back for the wedding. My brother-in-law had asked an old college friend called Sam to the wedding. She herself was living in New York at the time. At the dinner I sat next to her. She was great, not my usual type, but we got on really well. We talked about living in the States, and she told me that after London she was going to LA to see some friends. We agreed to meet up and exchanged telephone numbers.

Sitting at the airport the following Monday I found myself thinking about her. I didn't know why really, but I couldn't get her out of my mind. I kept thinking how I would love to see her right now. I was about to check the departure board when I suddenly saw her struggling through the terminal with her trolley and cases. I couldn't believe it. I hadn't asked her when she was flying to LA at the wedding. It was an unbelievable coincidence – although I'm sure Rita would say it was fate!

I rushed up to her and said hello. She checked on to my flight and we went for a coffee. We got on so well we talked the whole way back to LA. It was as though we were old friends. When we arrived in LA her friends were waiting to pick her up. I didn't want her to go. I went to kiss her goodbye hoping that she would suggest meeting up the following day when she suddenly kissed me on the mouth. Not a long kiss, but a real one.

That was that. I called her the next day, as soon as I woke up, and we started seeing each other. She moved to LA last year and we are now living together. We haven't discussed marriage; sometimes I think it's

> *because we don't need to. I don't need to walk down an aisle to know that she is my soul mate.*

Had Peter not gone back to America he would never have found Sam when he did. His spirits made him come back here first to realize what was going on though. They had to make him go through a painful time so that he would move back to America, and through that journey meet Sam.

One of the greatest misconceptions of all is that we can change people. We can't. People go through phases and have characteristics that are stronger and more prominent at certain phases of their lives, such as low self-esteem, shyness, and enthusiasm. But on the whole we stay the same. What happens to a lot of people who are having affairs of the heart is that when they first meet a partner they fall head over heels in love. They think that this is it, that they are in love and that they want to be with that person for ever. They have just met and they spend a great deal of time in each other's company getting to know one another.

At this stage in the relationship they cannot imagine their partner doing wrong; they love, or at least they think they do, everything this person does or says. But as time wears on our perception of people changes; as we get to know them better both parties start to display their true selves. And then a horrible moment takes place when one, or both of you, look at the relationship and think, 'This is not right,' 'She is not the one,' or 'He is not the man I thought he was.'

When you first meet your soul mate you should feel that you could spend the rest of your life with them. That no one else on the entire planet matters. You cannot imagine spending a day apart from them. You should not be thinking that if they were a bit more easygoing or more sensitive things would be heavenly. You have to learn to be accepting in your relationships, even with your soul mate, which is something I will address in the next chapter. You cannot change a person, you can only grow with them. Therefore, if there are characteristics in your partner you think you cannot live with, and want to change if things are to continue, then you are not with the right person.

Your spirit will not send you someone you cannot get along with. More often than not you are confusing passion or infatuation with true love. Conversely, if you find that you are 'settling' for the way a person is, 'putting up with things', then you have not found your soul mate.

Janice had been living with her partner Matt for seven years. Matt was a very self-opinionated young man. As Janice said to me, it was either 'his way or the highway'.

Janice, on the other hand, was a very sweet and easygoing girl. She had put up with Matt's behaviour for a while but recently his attitude had really begun to get to her. She had always thought that he was 'the one'. But she could no longer stand the way he was behaving, and when she came to me she was very seriously contemplating leaving him.

At once Janice's grandfather, Robert, came through to me. He was watching out for Janice and felt that she should leave Matt as soon as she could. Matt, he told me, would never change and he would never marry her. He told me that Janice was living in Matt's house, that everything belonged to him and that he made her very aware of that. He told me that whilst Janice and Matt did have good fun together he hurt with his selfishness. Matt could never let Janice win an argument because in his mind he was always right. Robert told me who her soul mate was and that he shared the same initials as Matt.

I see this pattern quite regularly with young people who get involved in serious relationships. When the infatuation and attraction have worn away they often find that there is nothing left. They find that their characters irritate each other. That the more accommodating a partner becomes, the more belligerent the other happens to be, and so on. As they grow up they realize that they are with the wrong person, but they feel that they must be with their soul mate, because they have been together for so long.

If this situation sounds familiar to your own, step back from the relationship and ask yourself the following questions:

- Is this *really* a good person for you to be with?
- Are they making you happy?

- Do you find that you are making excuses for their behaviour towards you?
- Do they respect you and your opinions?
- Do you really like this person for who they are?

You see, there is a big difference between accepting that you and your partner have differences, and putting up with behaviour that you would not tolerate from your best friend. Soul mates argue and can have serious problems together, which we will look into later on, but theirs is a love that can conquer all sorts of difficult times and situations. If a relationship is going to stand the test of time there must be understanding, mutual respect, and friendship.

People who have found their soul mate very young are lucky. This tends not to happen very often. Through my work I come across so many wonderful people who feel that they have failed because they have not yet found their soul mate, and they want to know why. They believe that because they didn't find their soul mate early in life there must be something wrong with them. There isn't. The fact that you didn't meet your soul mate when you were in your twenties has no relevance to the person you are. There is no optimum age to fall in love. You find your soul mate when you are ready.

No one should feel inadequate if they have a history of broken relationships behind them, or because they have not yet married. It is better to have been testing the water with others than to marry and to be very unhappy.

It is not a reflection on you that you haven't found the right man or woman yet.

I cannot begin to tell you how many beautiful, kind, warm, clever, charming people there are in the world who have struggled to find success in relationships. They are so desperate to find love they cling on to the relationships they do have right till the bitter end in the hope that they will improve. They convince themselves that they are in love when they aren't, that they have found their soul mate when they haven't.

This is because having never known the deep binding love that exists between soul mates, they have nothing with which to compare their feelings. They stay in these relationships because they convince themselves that their relationship is much better than it is. They pretend to others and to themselves that their partner has attributes and qualities that are not there.

People try to work at these relationships. They think that a romantic meal in a restaurant, or a holiday for two will give them the time they need to make love grow. Of course, given the right surroundings most relationships will blossom. Spending time with each other alone, enjoying activities together and sharing thoughts and ideas can all help. But you cannot force the love you have to become as intense or intimate or as fulfilling as the love between soul mates. You either have it with someone or you don't. It's as simple as that! I recently spoke to a lovely girl called Amanda who was in a relationship like the one I have just described. She had convinced herself she had found true love when she hadn't. This is her story.

AMANDA

I had been seeing my boyfriend James for six years. We met when I was twenty-seven through a mutual friend. After a year of going out we moved in together. I think I thought that this would make us closer, but if I'm honest now I think it just drove us apart. I would never have admitted this at the time because I was determined that we were right together. I wanted to marry James and convinced myself that we had reached the stage in our relationship when it was the right thing to do.

When I rang Rita Rogers for a reading it was not about anything like this. I had told myself I was very happy and lucky to be with James and I certainly did not need any advice on the subject. I rang Rita because I had seen an article about her in Australian Vogue *and I really wanted to speak to her. My sister died when I was a teenager and I had always wanted to believe that she was still 'around'. Although she was five years older than I was we were very close. I wanted to know from Rita what happened when she died, and whether she was OK now.*

I had heard that Rita was good but I was very surprised when she came out with my sister's name immediately. Caroline had been twenty-one when she was killed in a road accident. Rita told me, correctly, that Caroline had been on the back of a motorbike when it crashed. I was surprised by the amount of detail she could give me, not just about the accident but about our childhood and family, too. When we were growing up Caroline was a lot wilder than I was. She was always very cheeky and this came through in my reading.

Rita then asked me who James was. She said that Caroline was telling her that we lived together. She said she could see an apartment, which had a balcony, and that it was near water. This amazed me because our apartment was near Sydney harbour. She said it was a modern building, which it was, and that it was 'one big room'. Our apartment was open-plan.

I thought that Rita would tell me that we were soul mates and hoped she would give me a date when we would marry, that she might even tell me how many children we were going to have. But she didn't. What she said took me by surprise. She said that James and I were wrong for each other, that he wasn't my soul mate and that Caroline was saying to her that I deserved better. My initial reaction to this was shock. I wanted to think that she had made a mistake but deep down I knew she hadn't because what she had said about Caroline had been so accurate.

Rita told me that James was a nice man but that he was 'all wrong' for me. She then told me that we argued a lot, that we were making each other unhappy and that he frustrated me. This was in fact true. For some time James and I had been going through a very bad time together. We fought a lot and I found it very draining. I am quite ambitious by nature. I like to be busy and to work hard. But James wasn't like that at all. He liked to lie around, work only when he had to, and to spend his weekends getting drunk with his friends.

Rita said that James was a good person, but he had a lot of growing up to do and that he was not ready for commitment. She said that Caroline was saying that I had some money saved, which I did, and that I was going to use it as a deposit for an apartment. She said that this new apartment would have a view of trees and a large garden. And during this time, through moving, I would meet my soul mate very quickly. She said that his initial would be 'N'.

James and I did break up, and I moved out of our apartment. I live now in a first-floor flat that looks out on to a park. I found the place through a girlfriend. She knew about it because she had a colleague in the building. His name is Nick.

I have yet to meet this Nick, and I am intrigued to know if he is my 'N'. I am not even sure if I am ready to meet anyone else just yet. But what I am now sure of is that James was not my soul mate. This is not just because of what Rita said, I know this now from spending time on my own. I think that because of my age, and because I was scared of admitting that James and I were not right for each other, I convinced myself that he was the one and that we had a future together. I now know that it would never have worked and that I was fooling myself. Rita said to me during the reading that no relationship is a waste of time. I don't regret my time with James but I am glad that I now realize that it was not right for me.

Old habits die hard; often we stay in relationships because they are a habit. We are scared of leaving what we know. We think that because we have been with someone for a long time, because we have lived with him or her and have shared a life together that it must be right. Often it is not. We must have the courage to move away.

What scared Amanda was the idea that she had failed, that people would judge her if she admitted that it wasn't right. She was scared because she was in her mid-thirties, scared because she shared his friends and his flat and could not imagine a world without all of that. If you have the courage to say something is not right, if you are honest with yourself, you will be one step nearer to finding fulfilment with yourself, and eventually with your soul mate.

Unfortunately there are a great many people for whom love is not reciprocated. You imagine that you are deeply in love with a person, put everything you have into loving and caring for them but you do not get anything in return. You may have been in a relationship with that person and it did not come to anything or it may be that you loved them from afar but they never took any notice of your feelings, or if they did, they chose to ignore them.

Anyone in this position should not be disheartened. Hard as it may seem, you must face up to the fact that love is not there. However difficult it may seem, they were not right for you. You must try to put things behind you and not lose heart. It may be that you have convinced yourself that you were in love with them when you weren't. And even if you did *love* them, I can assure you that you were not *in* love with them. You may not understand this now but when you meet your soul mate, which you will, you will understand instantly what I am saying. The love between soul mates is a mutual love. It is never one-sided. There is no use in trying to make a person love you because they won't and even if you both try for a time eventually the relationship will come to an end. Wait for true love to come your way because when it does, you will wonder what you ever saw in this person in the first place. Sometimes we convince ourselves that we have a future with a person when we don't. Being told that you are not 'the one' can be very hurtful and can affect your self-esteem. But it is better to have been freed from a relationship that has no promise than to stay in it until it is too late. This is what Cathy discovered:

CATHY

It was a nasty break-up. It must have taken about two years for me to get my confidence back. I met my last boyfriend when I first went to university and we had been together for eight years when he suddenly said to me one night that he didn't want to get married. I thought he meant that he never wanted to marry anyone. That he didn't believe in it.

We had reached a stage in our relationship where it was time to take things forward. If he didn't want to get married how about we moved in together then? I looked at the floor. 'I don't think you understood what I was saying,' he said. 'I think it's over between us.' I was absolutely devastated. My world fell apart there and then. I could not believe that this man with whom I had shared my adult life was now saying this.

It was a hard time, but it also served as a very good lesson for me. At the time I thought I had wasted my life on this man and I felt a fool, now I don't see it like that. I think in a way this awful time taught me who I was and I am beginning to understand and like who I am now. I am far more myself than I was in that relationship, I am much braver and more light-hearted.

When it was all over, my work improved. I was posted abroad, and I met a man on a business trip with whom I got on really well. When I returned I called him up, something I would never have done before. Rita has said he is my soul mate, and I really feel that he is. I am such a different person now to who I was before. And I am glad that the break-up happened, because if I had carried on with that man I would never have become myself or found Daniel.

People often say when love doesn't work out, 'It was not meant to be.' I think that there is a great deal of truth in this. You are meant to be with a person who loves you as much as you love them. The fact that a relationship breaks down is part of fate. You have to leave that relationship so that you are free to find your soul mate. Remember that sometimes to appreciate real joy in life we have to have known pain.

As I have said before there is no optimum age to find your soul mate. If you have not found your soul mate yet – take heart. Over the years I have met many people who didn't find their soul mate until they were much, much older but when they did find them they all told me that it was worth the wait!

True love can come to us at any stage. There are some of us who just aren't ready for love when we are young. Just as some people are late developers, some of us are late when it comes to love and marriage. Nevertheless, just because love comes to us later on, that does not mean that it is any less intense or fulfilling than if we had found it when we were twenty-five. September relationships can be very rewarding. After all, a person who finds their soul mate after middle age has a lot to bring to the relationship. An older person is often more self-assured, content, fulfilled; they have probably done all the things they wanted and needed to in life already, so they can be much easier to settle down with.

Of course, finding love when you are old can be hard because we then have fewer opportunities to meet people. We get out less, we think perhaps that we should be spending our time and our money on our families. We think that it wouldn't be right for us to start gallivanting around town at our age. We think we should stick to the rocking chair and slippers rather than make fools of ourselves.

But in my mind there is no retirement age when it comes to love. True love is about the soul and your soul is ageless. Of course we may not be as sprightly as we were when we originally went courting but that should not stop us. Love knows no bounds. So your bones may be a bit creaky, you can't leave the house without your glasses and you can travel for free on the buses, but deep down you are just the same as you were when you were twenty-three. Your soul mate will love you for your soul regardless of your age. We all need love, and if you haven't found it yet, keep looking.

My advice is get up and get out of the house and stop worrying about your family and grandchildren. They are capable of looking after themselves, and would probably be much happier if you were living your life and enjoying it than sitting at home feeling your age! And after all, it seems being in love is one of the best health and beauty treatments there is. Falling in love will take years off you.

In my work I come across many older people who have not found their soul mate. This is usually because they married the wrong person when they were younger, out of convention, and lived their adult lives in a loveless relationship. If this has happened to you, don't give up hope just yet. For, like Sylvia, it may not be too late:

SYLVIA

I married very young. I was just nineteen. This is a terrible thing to say, but I know now that I was never really in love with my husband. Back then girls got married. You didn't hang around waiting for Prince Charming – you got an offer and took it. Women did not have the opportunities girls have today, either. You were educated to a point, but you weren't expected to use it. I worked in a shop for pocket money until I was married. I would not have called it an income; marriage was the only way out of your parents' house. When Jack came along and proposed I felt I had no alternative if I wanted to move on.

Our years together were fine. He worked hard, gave us a nice home and earned money to raise our three girls well. For many years I thought I was happy – I didn't know anything else, you see. I liked romantic fiction and going to the pictures, but I thought that love like that didn't happen to women like myself: it only happened to make-believe beautiful people.

My daughters grew up and started lives of their own. Two of them married but all three have careers – doing things they wanted to do. When they left my life was so empty. My husband rarely talked to me, or thought of me as anything else than a wife or mother, so if I decided to discuss what was going on in the world he would scoff or ignore me.

I decided to do something for myself and became a volunteer helper. I did some caring in the community, and taught arts and crafts to a group of handicapped people. My husband was not interested.

In 1997 my husband died of an unexpected heart attack. I carried on. At around the same time one of my daughters had been to Rita for a reading. Rita had said that she felt Jack there in the room, and he was saying that I would be OK, and that I would meet someone. He would have the initial 'M'. She said that this would be my soul mate. My daughter was upset by this. I suppose she expected that her father was my soul mate. She wasn't going to tell me, but her husband made her. I think he was a bit more detached from everything and could see that I had been lonely even in my marriage. He told my daughter I deserved some happiness. I didn't think anything of it at the time; it wasn't really my thing. But I was quite amused. 'Me? At my age?' I said.

> *I met Marcus through my arts and crafts lessons for the disabled. His adult daughter, Amanda, was a member of our group and he came in a couple of times to pick her up. We began a slow but good friendship. His wife had left him when Amanda was a toddler. She just couldn't cope.*
>
> *I invited Marcus on an outing with the arts and crafts group and that's when I realized that he was the man I had been waiting to meet all my life.*
>
> *I do not regret my marriage for an instant. I love my children more than anything in the world. But now I feel like I am being loved and I can return that love. I will be sixty-nine soon but that doesn't seem to matter. I feel like I'm thirty-five. I never thought that love like this existed outside of fiction but it does. My children now see what I have missed out on and they are no longer resentful that their father was not my soul mate.*

Whatever your situation, whatever your age, it is never too late to have a chance at love. For Linda, life began at fifty. She had suffered so many personal tragedies before this it was no wonder she had not found love before. She had lost her brother when she was just fifteen to leukaemia. And the following year her childhood sweetheart was taken from her in a road accident.

When he died Linda was terribly upset – she never really recovered. She never married and had a string of broken love affairs that left her unhappy. When she rang me for a reading a young man came through. He said that his name was Paul. I asked Linda if she knew him. 'Yes,' she said. 'He was my soul mate.' He told me how he died. 'Yes, yes,' said Linda, 'that is him. He is the reason why I have never married.'

But Paul was desperate for Linda to know that although he had loved her very much, and cared for her, visiting her from time to time, he was *not* her soul mate. Paul was telling me that Linda had yet to meet that man. Linda was very taken aback by this. 'That can't be!' she said. 'I'm afraid it is,' I told her. 'But you shouldn't be sad because you do still have a chance of finding true love and happiness now,' I said. Paul was telling me the initial of the man Linda would meet. He said that he would send him to her, and that he would come to her through her work.

Some months later he arrived on the scene, as promised. They are now living together, and Linda has her chance at happiness at long last.

Not everyone, of course, *wants* to find a soul mate in this life. There are a great many people who are quite happy and content being on their own. They do not feel the urge to share their lives with another person. They feel quite complete being by themselves. This is not to say that they do not have a soul mate – as I have said before, we *all* have one. What it means is that they will not meet their soul mate on this earth plane.

There are two reasons for this. For some people this

is because their soul mate may have gone before them, before they ever had the chance to meet them. They may have been taken before their time in a tragic accident, for example. It could be that they were just not destined to meet in this life. Fate may not have brought them together but they have not lost out on love, because they will meet them eventually.

When this happens I find that the soul mate left here, although unaware that this is the case, comes to the decision that they are quite happy being on their own. They are adamant that they will never marry – even though they might have wanted to in the past – and say that they are happy as a bachelor or spinster. However, as soon as they reach the spirit world when they die, they will be united with the soul mate who was matched with them before they were even born.

For others, being on one's own is a conscious decision. Some very spiritual people decide that they do not need to have a soul mate in this life because they already have a deep union with their own faith. Priests, monks, nuns and other celibates tend not need to find a soul mate because they have already formed a spiritual bond with their God. People who by nature are very spiritual are in less need of finding love with another person because they already have peace within their souls. Again, this does not mean that they do not have a soul mate, it means that in this life they have chosen not to take one. But when they reach the spirit world, their soul mate will come to them.

There are many other sorts of people who do not find their soul mates here in this life. This may be because their lives are cut tragically short, because they never reach adulthood, because they are part of a generation lost to war. They may never find themselves in the right socially interactive situation, or want to trust another person that much. But whatever the situation, you should not worry, for whatever happens here, even if you spend your whole life on your own, in spirit you will be united with your soul mate. Your soul mate will be the same soul mate you were given before your birth and you will find them as soon as they reach the spirit world if you have gone before them.

FOUR

Letting Go and Moving On

Unfortunately, not all of us are lucky enough to find our soul mate early on in life and sadly there are a great many people who find themselves in relationships with the wrong person. Because of the many pressures we face today as individuals living in a modern world we sometimes feel that it is better to be with anyone than to be on our own. We worry that if we do not marry or commit to a relationship we may never find love or happiness. We think that if we are to have children and a family of our own we should take what we are offered rather than wait for Mr or Miss Right.

And so we find ourselves trapped in relationships from which we cannot escape. We know that we are unhappy and not fulfilled and yet we find it impossible to leave. We may pretend to others and to our families that everything is OK, that we are happy, and we may even try to convince ourselves that this is the case. Yet if you are honest with yourself you will realize that you are miserable.

Even though we may be aware of this at the time we find it difficult to move on. We create a long list of reasons why we should stay. You think about your children. You worry about how your partner would cope on their own. You worry how you might survive living by yourself, how you would manage financially, where you would live and so on.

However, what you should always try to remember is that you only have one life here, and it is important to try to make the most of it while you still can. If the person you live with makes you genuinely unhappy, takes you for granted or makes you feel worthless then it is time to leave that relationship. You may feel that it is too late, but you never know what will happen until you move on. For all you know the love of your life may be just around the corner.

Maggie wrote to me from Australia last year when her marriage broke down. She has written this story in her own words.

MAGGIE

I had been with Greg for twenty years, married for fourteen, when we separated last year. We were very young when we met and I was very idealistic. My mother is Italian and Catholic so I was brought up to think that marriage and family were more important than anything else in life. If you said to me even two years ago that I would end up getting divorced I would have been shocked. Divorce was never even an option for me. Divorce was for people who were too selfish and lazy to fight for their marriage. It would never be something that I would do.

That said I cannot pretend that my marriage was a success. We didn't have anything in common. Greg was quite a male chauvinist, he didn't believe that women should work, he believed that they should be there for the family. This was fine when we were young. I didn't mind being a housewife, we had two boys and I loved spending time with them. But after they grew up and left home I realized that there was nothing left for me. Greg ignored me. When we spoke it was because I had initiated the conversation and then it was only ever about the boys. I found myself becoming increasingly lonely even though I was married. If I got upset about this and told Greg what was happening to me he would shout at me and walk out. It was awful. My mother said I should get used to it. She said it was the menopause and that in time I would be happy again. But my friends thought differently. They knew how difficult Greg was, how he used to dismiss my opinions and make fun of me in front of other people. They thought it would be best, now the boys had gone, if I lived apart from Greg even if it was just for a while. I was not sure about this at all. The whole idea of separation for me equalled failure, but things had got so bad I used to dread going home in the afternoon in case my husband was there.

While I was away my appointment to speak to Rita came through. One of the first things that Rita said to me during that reading was that she sensed that I had just been separated from my husband. I didn't know how she could possibly tell this as I was speaking to her over the telephone but she said that my father, Brian, was talking to her from the spirit world. She said that it was a good thing that I had left my husband because, as she said, 'there is no love left in that relationship any more'. Rita said that she knew I was thinking of going back to him but was adamant that I should not. 'All the love between you has gone,' she said. 'If you go back you won't be happy.' Rita knew that I was forty-two and she correctly named my two boys. She told me what they were doing now, that one was studying to be a doctor and that the other was 'something to do with animals'. He is a zoologist.

Rita explained to me that my husband was essentially a good man but that I deserved better. She said that I had spent too many years of our marriage making excuses about the way he behaved to me and pretending to my family that we had the perfect marriage. She knew that I had been trying to make a go of it but it wasn't working out. Had anyone else told me any of this then I don't think that I would have listened to him or her. I think I would have said 'You don't know what you are talking about' and ignored their advice. But Rita had convinced me that she was for real. She said too many things to me that no one else knew about, so I felt that my father really must have been talking to her. She knew, for instance, that Greg had a drink problem, which he kept secret, which was true because I had recently found empty spirits bottles stashed away in the garage and in his study. She knew I had had a miscarriage in between our boys and that my sister had had a cancer scare.

I asked Greg for a divorce in November 1998. (When I told him he didn't say a word, he didn't even look up from his paper.) I didn't do it because of Rita; I did it because I had been in an unhappy and loveless marriage for far too long. But the reading with Rita forced me to own up to a few home truths. She also made me see that I had a life outside of marriage. Rita told me that1999 would be my year. I hope she is right. I have started studying and have made some new friends. She said that I would meet my soul mate in 2000 and that his name will be Steven. Who knows what will happen in the future. For the moment I am very happy as I am.

Like so many people who come to me for readings, Maggie found it difficult to accept that her relationship was over. For years she had tried to convince herself that it was not as bad as it seemed and that it would get better in time. But the simple fact was that for Maggie and Greg the love had gone and when you are not soul mates there is never any chance of trying to get it back. A great many people end up in unhappy relationships because they believe in marriage more than they believe in love. By this I mean they lose sight of what is really important. Marriage may give you security and stability but only love can bring you true happiness.

Maggie's situation is not uncommon. There are a great many people belonging to an older generation who because of social circumstance married young. Back then we didn't have the chance to get to know many people before we got engaged. We didn't even know our prospective husbands and wives that well either. In my day it was impossible for a girl to have any life outside of her home. You couldn't have proper boyfriends. You couldn't stay out at night. You were not supposed to be seen to be having a relationship with anyone unless you were married. It just wasn't the done thing.

We had no choice but to marry young. In those days you moved from your father's house to your husband's. My marriage to my late husband Dennis took place in 1957 when I was just sixteen. Although we ended up loving each other very much, and had four wonderful daughters together, I can honestly say now that initially my marriage was more of a release from my father's rule than a happy union with my new husband.

There are generations of people alive who are trapped in unhappy marriages because of social or external pressures. Many people got married either young or quickly because of the two World Wars. They did so because they had no idea whether they would ever come back and they wanted a chance at happiness, however brief it would be. There was a sense of urgency about it, men wanted to leave their mark on the world before they died. Until very recently many people also married because of pregnancy. They could not live with the stigma of bringing an illegitimate child into the world. Many women had no choice other than to get married. Back then a woman might have had a job but she certainly did not have a career. Getting married gave a woman financial security. As a result, I have come across a great many men and women through my work who are trapped in marriages with people with whom they share nothing more than a history and children.

Things are very different today and I think that young people are extremely lucky. It is no longer socially important to be married. A woman can be independent, financially secure and have a career of her own. Women today do not need to get married. These days they do so because they *want* to not because they are forced to. The invention of the contraceptive pill has meant that many couples are able to enjoy their relationships without having to commit themselves to marriage or children. They can live with their boyfriends and girlfriends and get to know who they are as people before they commit themselves to each other for life. And even if a child is conceived there is no social stigma about bringing a child into this world outside of wedlock or being a single parent. And so with all of these changes people are less likely to be locked into loveless unions and are free to look for their soul mates. As I said, they are very lucky.

Should you feel trapped in a relationship or locked into a loveless marriage you should not despair. You should never give up hope for there is a strong chance that you will eventually meet the person with whom you are really supposed to be in this life. But to do this you need to let go and move on.

Letting go from a relationship, from the person you have spent part or all of your adult life with, takes great strength and courage. It is not an easy step. It is not something you should do on a whim, either. You should only do it if you are sure that you are unhappy and that it is the relationship you are in that is responsible for making you feel this way.

I find that a lot of people who are in the unhappiest of relationships stay only because they think that they aren't strong enough to get out and because they assume that when they are on their own they will feel even worse. You must realize that by finding inner strength you can carry on, and that there is always hope for the future. This is not your lot. You may have been destined to go through a bad time, to be in this relationship, but you are also destined to know real love and happiness with a soul mate.

If you feel unhappy with your partner, if you cannot bear the relationship you are in, then get out. You are not with your soul mate. You may think you are because you have been married for twenty-five years, so therefore you qualify, but if they are making you miserable then I can assure you that they aren't the one for you. You may be married all your life to someone who isn't necessarily your soul mate. A husband and wife who are joined by a legal tie in this life but who share no spiritual bond and who were mentally divorced from each other will not be together in the next. They will each be united with a soul mate whether they met them here or not. As I have said before, when we reach the spirit world we only go to those we love.

Although it may not feel like it when it happens, breaking up with someone you do not love can be a very positive step forward. There may be a lot of heartache and pain involved in ending a relationship but it is worth it. Think of it not as an end but as the beginning of the rest of your lives. I believe that spirits sometimes intervene when relationships go sour and that they try to show us the way out. Just as spirits can lead us to our soul mates, they can also reveal situations to us that serve as catalysts and lead us out of our relationship. For example, when you walk in on your husband with another woman, when you discover empty alcohol bottles hidden under the sink or find something you shouldn't in your partner's coat pocket you do all these things because you were supposed to. These things do not happen by chance, they are signs sent to you by the spirits who love you. They do this because they love you, they are not trying to hurt you, they just don't want to see you deceived.

Discovering that your partner has been unfaithful to you can be extremely sad and painful. You feel betrayed and hurt. You may begin to feel worthless and rejected. You may feel that your life and the meaning of your life are over. If this happens to you, you must move forward and be strong. Another person's infidelity is not your weakness, it is theirs. If they are not your soul mate then my advice to you would be to let go and move on. However much in love you thought you were with that person you will discover when you do find your soul mate that it is nothing in comparison to the love you will share in the future.

A relationship that has turned nasty or sour can leave us with a bad taste. We start feeling tired, we suffer from a lack of self-esteem, we feel depressed. During that time we lose our strength, we become introverted, weakened and full of negative feelings. You may feel that you will never be mentally strong enough to cope with another relationship ever again. But in time you will get better, your spirits will come to help you, to guide you to a happier place, towards people who will love and care for you.

Often when we are in a relationship that is not going well, we find it easier to bury our heads in the sand rather than face reality. The thought of living on our own, of surviving without our partner can be a terrifying prospect. Humans are creatures of habit, we get attached to people and ways of life however bad they might be and so we stay where we are. I never think this is a good idea for anyone to do. I'm afraid that sometimes we just have to face the music and say goodbye.

If you stay in a relationship where neither of you is happy no good can come of it. You may be able to ride it out for a while but in the end you will start destroying each other. One of you will become resentful of the other and damaged by the lack of respect, warmth and love. We should only ever be in a relationship when it is a good one. Of course, many relationships, even those between soul mates, can go through bad phases; you must learn to recognize the difference between a phase and a situation that has no silver lining.

It does take courage but it is important for your own self worth to get out. There is only so much that a person has to take in life. Laura had taken about as much as she could when we met. She approached me when her life was turned upside down by her husband's behaviour.

LAURA

We had been together for ten years when my husband turned round to me one day and said in a very matter of fact way that he didn't love me any more. I was stunned. I knew that things had been difficult for a few years but we were coping and I thought that we were happy. When he told me he didn't love me I was so wounded. I spent that whole day sitting there staring into space wondering what was wrong with me, what had I done wrong. I felt worthless, that I had failed as a wife, a mother and as a woman. I had thought that we would always be together. Until this point he had always been a very caring husband and father. 'This cannot be happening to me,' I kept thinking. It was as though I were watching someone else's life in a film.

In the weeks preceding this bombshell my husband's behaviour had become quite strange. He had been very ill-tempered and snappy. He then started getting these headaches and saying that he kept dreaming about hurting his family. He then said that he was going to go away, that he could not stand being here and that he wanted to be on his own. He said he felt angry and that he was not sure if he could be happy anywhere.

I was so confused by this sudden change in my husband that I actually made an appointment to speak to Rita. I wanted to find out what was the cause of this problem. I suppose I rather naively thought I might be able to sort it all out when she told me what was wrong, and that he would then come back. But Rita didn't tell me what I wanted to hear. She told me the truth. She said that my husband was not my soul mate and that I must let him go. She said that he wanted his freedom and that I must let him have it not only for him but for myself as well. She told me that if I looked into my heart I would find that I was not actually very happy anyway, and that it would be very difficult to come to terms with at first. In time I would come to realize though, as I grew stronger, that he was not for me. I cannot say it has been easy, but Rita did also give me hope.

She told me that a man I knew already would enter my life and that slowly I would find true love with him. She said his name, and I think now she might be right.

The soul mate who came through for Laura is the man she should have been with all along. He is kind and warm, he would never hurt Laura or her children because unlike her husband he is full of love. When her husband left, although it was very difficult for Laura, everything gradually began to improve. The atmosphere in the house became happier and her children felt more secure and began to blossom. We imagine a two-parent house is better for children but it can be more damaging than we think, because if there is no love in the house, only anger, it will affect them.

Children need to be around love, and even if we do not tell our children how bad things have become they can detect it in our moods, our silences, our touch. We should not cling to things that make us so unhappy, to people who can be so hurtful and so abusive. You may think you want someone back, perhaps because it is easier that way, or because you don't think that you will ever meet anyone else. A break-up can destroy your confidence. But if you don't move on you will never find true happiness, either by being on your own or by meeting another person.

I have seen so many women who have been destroyed by men. They may not admit it at first because they feel ashamed, or because they are denying it to themselves, but you can see it in them. You don't have to be psychic, either! Their physical appearance gives it away. They hide their figures behind their clothes, because they have been made to feel worthless and unattractive. They behave nervously, blaming themselves, defending their marriages, apologizing a lot. And when you do tackle the subject with them, they tell you how they cannot leave, how they are sure that he does not mean it and so forth. But believe me, when they do leave, when they walk out of that door and see me six months later, they are new women, they are *themselves* again.

Rejection in a relationship is also very difficult to cope with, particularly when you have been married or in a long-term relationship with someone.

Andrea always knew deep in her heart that she would not grow old with her husband. Married young, they were divorced within six years, when Andrea was just twenty-eight. Her ex-husband remarried quickly and this was hard on Andrea, not just because she felt rejected herself, but because he gave up custody of their four-year-old son Sam in the process and said he didn't want further involvement in his life.

Andrea found it hard to cope. As she said to me, 'To turn your back on your marriage is one thing, but to turn your back on your child is unforgivable. 'What broke her heart most was the fact that Sam kept asking when Andrea would remarry. He said he wanted her to, because he wanted to have a new daddy. She began seeing someone else and had a brief affair, but it ended when he went back to his ex. By this stage Andrea could take no more.

Two rejections in a very short space of time are difficult to deal with. But I felt that with Andrea the second rejection could have been avoided. What Andrea wanted was not the man but the relationship; this one would have never worked out.

When I read for her, her spirit guides told me that her husband would come back, which they said she must avoid at all costs. This relationship would not last, he would always leave again, which would be hard not only for Andrea but also for her child. They said that she should not worry though, because she had a wonderful soul mate. they gave me his name and they said she would be able to trust this man with her life, and I know that he will come along when the time is right.

When someone is in a violent relationship people often think that they should just get out. 'How can they stay, how can they love their partner when this goes on?' they ask each other. Relationships that are violent are often very complex. Often the victim of abuse will try to deny that there is anything going on in the first place. They usually try to find excuses for the way their partner behaves blaming the pressures of work, for example, financial difficulties or alcohol abuse. There is no excuse for this kind of behaviour. It is totally unacceptable and anyone suffering from this kind of mental or physical abuse should try to leave that relationship as quickly as possible. It won't get better: that person will not reform, and it will do a great deal of damage to your confidence.

The fact is that a person who treats someone else in this way is not their soul mate. Whatever difficulties you might have in a relationship with someone you truly love, violence and abuse should never enter the equation. Our soul mates would never hit us or do anything that would intentionally hurt us or cause us distress.

Jemma wanted this story to be published to help all those like her who feel that they are trapped in violent relationships from which they might never escape.

JEMMA

The day I met Rita Rogers she gave me the first ever glimmer of hope in my life. I was in a very violent marriage to a man who would threaten to hurt anyone I told about the way he abused me. He said he would go after my father, who was the closest person to me, if I ever told him what I had suffered. And he meant it. At that point in my life the only way out of my situation I could see was suicide.

Rita was very kind to me. I told her nothing about what was going on in my life at first, but she said that my grandmother was telling her about me anyway. Rita knew my life story, everything that my husband had done to me, things she could not have possibly found out from anyone else because I had never told a soul what went on in my marriage. It was too personal, and it made me feel ashamed.

The reading must have gone on for over an hour when Rita asked me who John was. I said that John was my brother's name. Rita paused and gave me a wry smile. 'Oh no, this John is not your brother, this John works with you.' John and I had worked in the same company, and for some time I knew that there was a mutual attraction but that was all. I could not have hoped for anything more, not in my circumstances.

But Rita had told me that I would escape my husband in November and that by March the following year I would be divorced. At the time I could not believe what I was hearing. My husband would surely not let me go, and how could I be able to obtain a divorce that easily? Rita then said that I was destined to spend my life with John, that in February we would be together, and within five years we would be married! I left Rita dreaming of what she had said, but I did not really believe that it would come true. I went back home that night to my miserable life.

As the year went on my marriage got worse and the beatings became more frequent and more brutal. One evening my husband went for me, but this time I managed to escape from him. I ran to the car, got in it, shut the door and started it up. He was chasing me and smashing the windows with a crowbar as I started up the engine and drove off.

Blinded with tears I drove and drove. I did not know where to go, but knew I could never return. I don't know what possessed me but I found myself outside John's flat. I rang his doorbell. When he answered the door he was delighted to see me. Then he saw the bruises. He hugged me and did not say a word. We talked for most of the night, me confused and shaken, him calm and reassuring, listening all the time. The next day he drove me to my sister's. It was November.

Needless to say Rita was right. By February that year John and I were living together. On 27 February the first part of my divorce came through. John and I grew stronger and stronger as a partnership as time went on. I never knew I could feel so happy. In time, the divorce was finalized. Some time later, we reached a point at which we thought we should start a family, and we decided to get married.

At the wedding, one of John's aunts asked how long we had been together. I smiled as I answered 'Five years.'

However bad things get in life, however bad your marriage, relationship or divorce are, never lose sight of hope. Our spirits cannot prevent bad things from happening to us but they can make our lives better. As Grandma Alice said to me when I was a child, 'Whatever harm comes to you, I'll reverse it.' Harm *has* come to me in my life, sad and awful things have taken place that have caused me hurt and pain, but as my grandmother promised, they have been reversed. For everything bad that has happened, some good has come in its place. Jemma's spirits could not take away the physical pain of the beatings she suffered at the hands of her husband, but they took away the other pain by bringing her soul mate John to her and by giving her children. Whatever you are suffering now, however bad things have got at home, remember that there is hope and believe that one day, like Jemma, your hope may become your reality.

FIVE

Follow Your Heart

If you are looking for true and lasting happiness in life then I have only one piece of advice: always follow your heart. You see, I think that we can only really be truly happy in life when we are loving, being loved or have known love. There is nothing more important in life than love, there is nothing more rewarding, nothing more fulfilling. We all want it, we all need and we deserve it.

I always say that this life here, on earth, this is your hell. You will never know anything worse than this life. But the one thing that can make it better, that can make sense of it all, that can give us reason to carry on, is love. Love gives meaning to life, which is why we spend our lives searching for it.

If you turn your back on love, decide to live without it or never make any room for it in your life you will never be fulfilled as a person. So in order to be fulfilled and happy you must follow your heart.

However, this is not always as easy as we would wish it to be. For a multitude of reasons sometimes we cannot go with our heart. It is often difficult for us to follow its desire. There are some people who will never be able to go where love is in their lifetime. But for others, if you have the strength and will, it is possible and important to go with your heart and soul.

Life would be much easier if we all met our soul mates when were in our early twenties. It would be a perfect and much happier world if we could marry our soul mates young and were therefore content and happy with that person for the rest of our lives. But as we all know life does not work that way.

Many people do not meet their soul mate until much later in their lives. This could be for a number of reasons. It may have taken you a long time to discover who you really are and what you want. It may be because you were destined to concentrate on your career first. Or it could just be that you and your soul mate kept missing each other, for one reason or another you kept failing to meet.

This would be fine if we remained single or unmarried, but it is usual for people to reach a stage in their lives when they are fed up of waiting for 'the one'. What happens to many people is that they no longer believe that there is such a thing as true and lasting love. They give up on the notion altogether, believing that it will never come their way.

People in these circumstances often end up compromising. Whether they realize it or not they are settling for second best. They do this for a multitude of different reasons: perhaps because they do not want to spend their lives on their own, perhaps because they want to start a family. And so they settle for the first person that offers them a future.

People who do this may love the partner they are with, but they are not *in* love with them, even if they have convinced themselves that they are. I have nothing against people who choose this path. Sometimes I think it can be a very sensible thing to do. Out of these relationships come many great things, such as wonderful children. It can also be healthy for people to be in relationships rather than struggling through life on their own in the hope that one day their true love will come knocking on their door.

But people who do this should realize that these relationships can get complicated. Our soul mate may, for all we know, be lurking right around the corner. Furthermore, just because we are now in a stable relationship does not make us immune from falling in love. Indeed, the feelings we have for a soul mate that enters our life when we are already in a relationship often become more intense. This is because we know that we are not free to love, because we are unable to openly express our emotions for our soul mate and so the relationship we have with them becomes illicit and clandestine. However, don't use this as an excuse for a string of extra-marital affairs. The feeling I am describing is much more powerful and certain than that heady thrill.

Some soul mates are not able to be together because of these reasons. We feel that we should not go where our soul is because it is wrong, that there are people involved who will inevitably get hurt and suffer. They might know that their partner is not their soul mate, but they still love them and do not want to cause them unnecessary hurt or pain.

But by not being honest about how we feel about someone we can, in the long term, do more harm than good. People who do this usually end up very unhappy because they spend their lives thinking about what could have been. Sometimes things are so bad that soul mates who cannot be together feel they have to stop seeing their true love altogether if they have any hope of making their lives bearable. But as the following story shows, this is not always the case.

JULIE

My name is Julie and I have just turned forty. I was in my mid-thirties when I agreed to marry Paul. I had known him for two years and we had met through mutual friends. I liked Paul a lot but not in a romantic way. We were good friends at first. He used to take me out from time to time and, as I was single, he was good to have around: he would always accompany me to parties and events. All of my friends were married and I don't have any brothers or sisters. This can be hard if you are on your own because married people only seem to know other married people and when you're with them all they talk about is their kids. I suppose meeting Paul was a blessing in that way.

I knew he always liked me but I did not feel the same way about him. I always clung on to the idea that I would meet 'someone' one day, and I would just know that he was the one for me. But as my thirty-fifth birthday drew nearer I began to give up hope. None of this was made any easier by my mother, who was desperate to see me settled with a nice man and a couple of children. Being an only child put even more pressure on me. I had not met anyone new for years, and I began to realize I probably never would.

So I started actually going out with Paul. We had a good time together and it surprised me how good it felt being part of a couple. When Paul asked me to marry him the day after my thirty-fifth birthday party I said yes. 'Why not?' I think was my reply – not very romantic, I know! A year after our wedding, to my mother's delight, I gave birth to our daughter Kelly. I gave up my full-time job and started temping so I could spend more time with the baby. And it was on a temping job that I met Justin.

Justin worked in the office where I was temping. I bumped into him as I was coming out of the car park. In fact, I nearly ran him down! I was in such a hurry to get back for the childminder that I backed out of my parking space straight into him. He was OK but I had knocked a box of papers out of his arms. I rushed to help. He was actually laughing – I don't think he could believe anyone could be so bad at driving. As I looked at him I just knew that there was something about him. It's funny, because Paul is really much better-looking than Justin, who is quite small with mousy hair. But all I kept thinking about was how nice he looked when he laughed.

We became friends over the month I spent at that office. We would have coffee together and he would tease me about my driving. We got on so well. The more I saw him the more I thought about him. I tried to stop myself, but it was no good. One day Justin was acting very strangely at work. We went for coffee and he was very quiet, which was unusual. I asked him what was wrong. 'It's you,' he said. 'I can't see you any more.' I was shocked. 'What are you talking about?' I asked. 'You know what I'm talking about,' he said. 'You know I like you, I like you more than you know, but you are also married and have a baby. I don't think I can cope with being with you when we have no future together.' I sat there staring at my cup. I didn't know what to say. I was leaving the job the following day, and had been worried that I might not see Justin for a while, but now I was never going to see him again, and I couldn't bear it. I thought I was going to burst into tears so I got up to leave without saying a word. As I was moving away from the table, he grabbed my arm. 'Just tell me one thing,' he said, 'you feel the same way too, don't you?' I don't know what came over me but instead of being honest I lied. Perhaps I felt my pride had been hurt. I'm just not sure. What I said was, 'I don't know what you're talking about,' and walked out.

I never saw Justin again. I was so upset I couldn't concentrate on anything. I loved him, he loved me, but he didn't want to be with me. There were times when I wanted to call but I didn't. I kept thinking to myself, 'you did the right thing, you're with Paul now.' And I threw myself into my home life. I arranged for Paul and me to take a holiday, thinking that it would make things better. But it didn't. Six months later I was even more miserable than I had been before. I decided to call Justin, but when I rang I was informed that he had left the company and had taken a job in America. The person at the other end of the telephone did not know where, or with what company – nobody knew where he was. That was two years ago.

I spoke to Rita last year when my mother passed away. She had breast cancer and had died suddenly. Her death had made me feel very alone. My mother came through immediately, which was very comforting. She talked about Kelly and Paul – Rita knew their names and knew that we were building an extension on to our house. Then Rita said, out of the blue, 'Who is J? I have a very strong feeling about this J. Is it Justin? Yes, it is.' She looked me straight in the eye and said, 'This husband of yours, Paul. He isn't your soul mate. Justin is.' I couldn't believe what I was hearing. I didn't say anything – I could barely speak, my mouth was so dry. Rita told me something about a car park, and a blue car. 'That's how you met,' she said. 'Soul mates always meet in strange ways, you know!' Rita knew that Justin was in America. 'He went because of you,' she said. 'He went because he felt you didn't love him.' And then to my further surprise she said, 'Why on earth did you lie to him?'

Rita told me that she didn't think Justin and I would be together in this life again but she said that we would be together in spirit. This has made it much easier for me to get on with my life now. I know that Rita is right – she must be, because she has been right so far about everything else. During my reading she also told me I was pregnant. I thought I wasn't, but she was adamant. She told me that I was going to have another little girl and that she would be born before the New Year. On 21 December last year Paul and I welcomed baby Natalie into the world.

For you to be happy in life it is very important to be true to your soul. Julie and Justin could have had a future together had she been honest with him. She gave up her chance with Justin when she pretended that she felt nothing for him, and her rejection drove him away.

However, Julie is lucky because she has two beautiful daughters and she does have Paul. Julie is also lucky because she has now known what true love is like. Julie and Justin are not fated to share their lives together, but they were fated to share the love they did, and which they will do again in spirit. But for this life, her marriage to Paul is a very good one. Ending it would be counter-productive. And both Julie and Paul will find their destined soul mates when they pass over.

Marriage is the most common reason why people who love each other are forced to live separate lives. There are a great many people in this world who have for whatever reason married the wrong person. It may be that they married too young or because there was a baby on the way. It may simply be because they thought they were in love with their spouse when in fact they weren't.

Realizing that the person lying beside you in bed is not your soul mate after all can be difficult to come to terms with. You may pretend that everything is all right. You may think that it is just a passing phase, but once you experience that feeling, the realization that you have made a mistake, you cannot get it out of your head. No amount of pretending or effort is ever going to convince you, or your spouse, that everything is rosy. We only have one soul mate. You cannot be soul mates to two different people.

Many people think that when this happens the right thing to do is to stay within that marriage. I disagree. The right thing to do is to be true, to be true to yourself and to be true to your partner. If you realize you have made a mistake, the best thing you can do is to leave that marriage. If you stay with your partner you will only end up resenting them. You may feel morally correct, but will you feel happy? In fact, by staying with them you are not doing them any favours. You are depriving them of a chance at true happiness with another person, with their *own* soul mate.

People may argue it is wrong to leave a marriage or relationship, and say that it is wrong to hurt the other person. But ask yourself, would you want to be in a marriage that your spouse was only staying part of because they felt obliged to *you*, because legally they were bound to stay with you?

If your spouse was deeply in love with another person, could you bear to be with them knowing that every time you put your arms around them they were thinking of someone else? Even if that person is not having an affair, they are cheating on you every day of your life in their head, just by even thinking about the other person!

Secondly, and as I have already said, staying with someone out of obligation means that you are depriving him or her of the chance of meeting someone else and finding happiness. Now, don't use this as an *excuse* to stray – I'm talking about something much more serious than that. And remember, physical love is part of the material world, not the spiritual matters we are discussing here. But I do believe, why be unhappy together when you would be happier apart, with people each of you is really in love with? You may think that you are being fair and kind to your partner, but are you? The fact is that even if they ask you not to leave because they love you, that you are their world and reason to live, you are not their soul mate. Soul mates do not have marriages like this. Soul mates' marriages are not one-sided. The feelings you have for each other should always be mutual. A soul mate does not fall in love with another person in the same rich way as they do with their soul mate: it is as simple as that.

Some people also think that they should stay within a loveless marriage 'because of the children'. They think that they are doing the right thing. Again, I think this is wrong. Look at the whole picture, of course. You must ensure that your children are adequately provided for, and staying together may be part of that. But don't create a negative environment for them, either. Children grow up. Even if your child is still a baby, in eighteen years it will be out of your door making a life for itself. Of course, don't think that they are going to thank you for what you have done. And by this stage it may just be too late for you or your spouse to start a new life with someone else. However, do you want to spend your life locked into a marriage with a man or woman who never speaks to you? Do you want to be in a marriage where you have grown apart to such a degree that you feel like strangers when you are together? Where the husband reads the paper, the wife sits there with her knitting, wondering what to say to each other? Do you want to go to bed every night with someone you cannot bear to touch? Or where once the children have left, you move into the spare room?

Children are also more perceptive than we sometimes

think. They pick up on an unhappy atmosphere in the house. Don't you owe it to them to create two happy homes rather than one tense, silent one? You can be a good mother, a good father, without having to live together. My advice to anyone in this situation is always the same. Sit down, talk to each other and put an end to the pain, silence and emptiness. Make two new lives for yourselves, and remain friends. It may be hard at first, but with courage you will discover, like Denise in the following story, that there is light at the end of the tunnel.

DENISE

I went to Rita for a reading some years ago. I had come to a point in my life where I could no longer cope with anything. I was suffering from depression and couldn't find any joy in my life. I had been married to Kenneth for fourteen years. We had three young children who were under ten at the time.

Kenneth and I had been going through a bad patch in our marriage. I say a 'patch', but in fact it had gone on for six or seven years. We argued the whole time about everything. As soon as I put the kids to bed at night it would start, and would continue until I had to get them up in the morning. I had hoped that by having another child our marriage would survive, but this was not the case. I don't regret having any of them, and I wouldn't change a thing now, but that was certainly was not the answer to our problems.

There was nothing particularly serious, not a sin-

gle event that I could say led to the breakdown of our marriage. There was no one else involved. It just didn't work out. I think that after years together both of us knew we had married the wrong person. We never said anything to each other but you could see it all over our faces. We brought out the worst in each other. With Kenneth I was irritable, unreasonable, and resentful. I think that he would admit to being sulky and distant. When we fought badly we would threaten each other with divorce, but neither of us ever meant it because we thought we should stay together because of the kids.

I went to see Rita because a friend recommended her to me. My father had passed away two years before and I wanted to talk to him. I think also because I was so low I wanted to know whether I was ever going to be happy again. Rita picked up my father in the reading. She knew how he had died, knew that he was called John, and that he had three sisters, all of whom she named. But the reading didn't end there. She told me that she knew I was unhappy and that I had felt this way for some time. She said that my husband 'K' was not my soul mate, but he was a good man and a very good father. She said that one day I would be happy, but not if I stayed in my marriage! She told me that one day my father would send me a man who would be my soul mate, but at the moment I must concentrate on getting my life back in order.

During the reading Rita described my house

perfectly, down to the pond at the end of our garden, and knew we had converted our garage into a playroom. But the thing that I will never forget is that she told me that our house was not a happy place. I thought she must mean that it was haunted or something. But she said that it was to do with Kenneth and me. She said that there had been many tears there, and that this was making our children unhappy. She said that my father was worried about Thomas, she thought he was having problems at school. Thomas is my eldest son.

I was, naturally, disturbed by what Rita said. When I went to pick up the children from school that afternoon I thought I would ask Thomas's teacher how he was doing. She said that she was glad I had come to her because she had been meaning to talk to me. She asked if everything was OK at home because Thomas had become very quiet at school and wasn't joining in with the other children during playtime.

That evening I decided that Kenneth and I had to sit down and sort things out once and for all. We talked properly for the first time in years! We agreed that whatever was going on between us was obviously having an effect on our children, which was unacceptable. We had to set aside our differences for them. Kenneth moved to a flat of his own shortly afterwards, and things improved. We got on better than ever but we also realized that we had no future together as husband and wife. It was all very mutual and grown up. We sold the house and both bought two smaller places. We agreed to share custody of the children and to do everything in a friendly way for them.

I now see Kenneth twice a week and we are acutally good friends. He has a great new girlfriend whom the children like, which is very important to me, and I have started seeing someone too. I am taking it slowly because I don't want to make the same mistakes again, but I am hoping that he might be the soul mate Rita said my father would send me.

One reason why some people end up with the wrong person is that they often don't know what they have until it disappears. This is very true of soul mates who meet when they are very young and are perhaps not mature enough to appreciate each other. Until it is too late, that is.

If your first ever relationship is with your soul mate, you do not have anything to compare it with. Often you end up taking the love and the closeness you have for granted because you may naively think that all relationships are like this. Naturally, this isn't true, but then you find yourself regretting what you have lost, and yearning to have it again.

Meg came to me at a point when she had reached a crossroads in her life and didn't know which path she should take. When she was in her late teens she had met and gone out with a young man called Luke. They had met at college and had fallen madly in love. For three years their relationship was extremely intense and passionate. But at the end of the third year they decided to put the relationship on hold. Luke was leaving college; he wanted to go away and travel. He told Meg that he thought they were too young to settle down. Meg always imagined that they would get back together and marry but by the time she had finished her course she discovered that Luke had found a new girlfriend and he had moved his things into her flat.

Eventually, Meg started a relationship with another man. They took a flat together and seemed happy enough. But then all of a sudden Luke started calling Meg out of the blue. He was having a few problems and he needed Meg to help him out. Meg was reluctant at first: she had not seen him for two years, he had had a baby with his girlfriend, and she was still angry with him. But Luke really needed Meg's support, and even though she was angry, Meg knew she still loved Luke. She agreed to help.

When I read for Meg I sensed at once that she was very confused inside. Her contact with Luke had made her realize that she was still deeply in love with him and that she did not feel the same way about her boyfriend. Her spirit guides were telling me that Luke was her soul mate and that in time they would be back together again.

When you have known true love like this it is impossible to escape from those feelings. When you are apart you can try to convince yourself you are over someone, but you never get over your first true love and as soon as you see them again all those feelings emerge.

Fate would bring these two back together. Whatever lives they had formed with other people would never compensate for the love they had known with each other. When you have been so close to someone it is hard to have that again with another person. This is why Luke called Meg when he was in trouble rather than turn to his girlfriend. Meg's spirits told me that she must be patient. Luke loved her but he would not come to her until he had sorted these problems out. In the meantime she must leave her boyfriend and find somewhere else to live.

Both her boyfriend and Luke's girlfriend would survive in the end. They would realize eventually that they were not with their soul mates either. Fortunately they were both young, so there would be time for them all to rebuild their lives.

Sometimes the thing that prevents us from being with our soul mate and following our heart is love itself. In so many cases parents, friends and family can stop their loved one from finding happiness. It is ironic because in most cases they think their influence will in the end increase their loved one's chances of finding true happiness. But often their intentions are misplaced.

Because of the nature of the love you have with your soul mate, people often do not understand what is best for you. With your best intentions at heart, they may say,

'Forget about that person, they are not right for you, you could do better.' But I think that only you really know what is best for *you*.

Just because a person is very close to you does not mean that they necessarily know what is best for you. No one else can ever really understand the essence of the love between two people – because they are not *those* two people. They cannot know what you see in that person. People around you may say, 'Why are you with them? What do you see in them?' Or they tell you that your soul mate is not good enough for you. But can they really know? They may be able to judge you because they know you; they may have opinions about your soul mate, but are they really in a position to question your relationship?

I am not saying you should ignore their advice. Realize that it comes with good intentions. Think about what they say and ask yourself if you are right about this person being your soul mate. Do not cut yourself off from these people because of their opinions. Remember that they are doing it because they love you. Listen to them, but always follow your heart.

A young lady called Frances came to see me when she was very upset about her boyfriend. He had been posted to the Far East. They had not known each other for more than three months when it happened. And yet during that time they had fallen very deeply for one another. Because of the brevity of their affair Frances had never had the chance to introduce him to her family or friends properly. And, furthermore, when he told her about the job opportunity over dinner one night she did not dare ask him where she stood.

FRANCES

As soon as he mentioned the posting I knew that this was the chance of a lifetime for Jim. The experience he would gain out there would set him up for life, and that it was something he had always dreamed about. Because of this I did not want to take anything away from his big moment. I didn't want to ask about where this left us. I just thought, 'Don't spoil it, let him have his moment and enjoy it.' After dinner, when we were going home, he said to me, 'You don't mind, do you?' I remember looking out the car window and saying, 'No.' It was not the truth.

As Jim made his plans to leave I went to see my sister and a good friend. 'Didn't he ask you to go with him?' they asked. 'No,' I said. They gave each other a look. They seemed to think that this was a signal, and that I should accept that the relationship was well and truly over. Had he loved me, he would have either stayed or invited me to go with him. I left lunch feeling very deflated.

When he went I was miserable for months. To make matters worse my sister started asking me to dinner parties where I was obviously the single girl. They were all trying to set me up. It was as if my affair and love for Jim were of no importance.

Jim and I talked on the telephone and wrote but it was not the same. A couple of times he asked me to come out and stay. I just wasn't sure. Everything my sister and friends had said kept coming into my head. His invitation seemed to be so casual.

One day when I went into work, there was a meeting going on. I asked the secretary what was happening. 'Don't you know?' she said. 'They're closing down your department.' Two weeks later I was called into the executive's office and made redundant.

I decided to take a holiday and I booked a package trip to Thailand. And I decided that en route I would spend a week with Jim in Hong Kong. When I told my mother she said that a girl of my age should not be chasing men who obviously didn't want to know me half way around the world. 'Leave it alone, forget him, he's obviously forgotten about you.' I'm sure she meant it with the best intentions, but I thought 'Well, if I don't go I'll never know.'

Just before I booked the tickets I had a reading with Rita Rogers. One of the first things she asked was, 'who is in the Far East?' I didn't reply, but she carried on. 'You must go there and be with him,' she said. I asked her why she thought that and she said that it was because we were soul mates. 'I know you are worried about it, but when you get there it will be perfect.' Rita then described a certain building and told me that my soul mate was called Jim.

Jim sounded very surprised when I told him of my

plans. I didn't know if he was pleased or not. When I arrived at the airport he was there. I thought on the long flight over that it might be strange and awkward, that I wouldn't now know what to say. But when we saw each other things could not have been more different. He flung his arms around me and was so pleased. We stood there in the airport holding each other and it was then I realized I had made the right choice.

He said that he had never dared asked me to give up my career, to move with him. He thought if he did so he would be being selfish, and he knew I was quite independent. The thing is, we had never really talked about how we felt about each other and so we had both felt very shy with each other. Had we known each other longer I think I would have gone straight out there. My parents' and my friends' views had also coloured the way I felt about him – I made myself very unhappy by listening to my family instead of my heart. I don't blame them because they didn't know him; if they had, they would have been able to see how perfect we are for each other.

We went from the airport out to dinner, and then on to Jim's flat. It was red and white with large views of the harbour – exactly like the space Rita had described. I never made it to Thailand. I spent a month with Jim in that flat in Hong Kong before we found a bigger place to move to together. I now have a job and am very happy. My sister came out here last month and said she was glad that for once I had listened to myself and not to her!

However, it isn't only parents and siblings who can be disapproving of our relationships. Children, I'm afraid to say, can be just as meddling! I'm not talking about babies, but adults. Just as our parents think that they know what is best for us, children often think they know best when it comes to their parents' well-being. Some children become so shocked and troubled when a parent falls in love with another person that they will go out of their way to prevent any union taking place between that parent and their new companion.

I received a letter from a very sweet pensioner called Albert. His wife had passed away three years ago and he wanted to know about his future. During his reading it came out that Albert and his wife had not been soul mates. I could tell this straightaway because his wife did not come through until right at the end of the reading.

Instead, Albert's brother Ronald came through and told me that Albert and his wife had not even been in love. They had only married because Penny, his wife, had been 'in the family way'. But then Ronald told me that Albert had now met someone whom he had fallen for. He said her name was Barbara, and that Albert wanted to marry her. This seemed wonderful because they *were* soul mates.

But when I spoke to Albert about this he seemed

rather flustered. I asked him if he did want to marry Barbara. 'Oh, yes,' he said. 'But I don't think that it is possible.' 'Why ever not?' I asked. 'Is she married?' Barbara was not married. That wasn't the problem. It was Albert's children that were in the way.

Albert had thought that his children would be elated when he told them that he had found a new 'lady friend' at the social club. But rather than being happy, they were dismayed, horrified even. They said cruel things about his age, and asked how he could do this to the memory of their mother.

The problem was that his children did not understand what their parents' marriage had really been like. They idolized Penny but they could not see that while, like so many women of her generation, she had been a very good mother, she had not been a good wife, and had never given Albert any love – just headache after headache. The poor man was in such a state: he didn't want to break their hearts by telling them the truth, he told me, but he wanted to be with Barbara.

I told Albert that he shouldn't worry about the kids. They were old enough now to take it, they had lives and families of their own, but *he* was alone. Love had come to him late in life, and he shouldn't waste any more time. He had to stop being a parent and be himself. Eventually, his children did see the light. Albert didn't have to say anything. I think they must have seen it themselves when they saw how happy he was with his new love.

*

It breaks my heart to think of all the people who are forced to deny how they really feel about each other because of circumstance. There are so many in this world who cannot be together even though they are deeply in love. Whether it is family, marriage, politics, war, or religion that keeps you from being together, always remember true love will conquer all.

Sometimes we cannot be with our soul mate; it just physically is not possible. I am not talking here about people who cannot be together because one is already married, or a soul mate who disappeared from your life but who you would find again. I am talking about those soul mates that become separated because of war, politics or imprisonment, people who have been forced to make the ultimate sacrifice: to give up their love because of intractable circumstances. The only consolation I can give here to those people is that true love will win out. The love between soul mates transcends everything. Even if you are only together for a short time, remember that no one can ever take that away from you. You always have your memories, the knowledge that they are still loving you, and the promise that when you both pass away you will be together for ever.

People may say to you that you will 'get over' someone, that time is a great healer, but I am afraid to say that simply is not true when it comes to soul mates. When you really, truly love another person you cannot turn that emotion on and off like a tap. You never get over your soul mate. You will think about them every single day for the rest of your life. There is no magical cure for this sort of love, and often I find that time may just intensify the feelings you had in the first place. But remember the consolations: you did enjoy true love together, your soul mate will visit you from the afterlife whether you know it or not, and you will be reunited there. And as I explain later, you soul mate may themselves arrange companionship for you in the meantime. But my advice is always, where possible, follow your heart. You are not on this earth for very long so always go with love.

No one on this earth should be forced to be with anyone they do not love. It is as simple as that. With the greatest respect to those cultures who believe in arranged marriage I am afraid that I cannot condone them and my heart goes out to all those who have been forced into loveless marriages by their families. As a parent I know we all want what is best for our children. We may think that our child will be safer and happier with a person from a similar background to our own, from a family that we know and like, and with a person who is going to offer them a safe financial future. But I would not want any of these things for my own children if it were to be at the expense of their own happiness. Over the years I have read for many Asian girls who have been forced into such arrangements. I have sat and listened to them cry and cry, as they tell me how they don't want to go through with their marriages.

Meena came to me some time ago in a terrible state.

She was a beautiful and intelligent girl, in her twenties. Although she was Indian by background she had been born and brought up in England. I did not know it at the time, but she was weeks away from a marriage her father had arranged when Meena was just a child. The man she was due to marry was coming over from India the following week. She had never met him. I didn't know any of this at the start of the reading.

Meena was very tight-lipped. There was only one question in her mind and that was who her soul mate was. Immediately his name came to me, but when Meena heard it she started to cry. I was correct: it was someone with whom she was very, very much in love. But it was not, of course, the man she was due to marry in two weeks' time.

Meena's soul mate was a Pakistani, although like Meena he had been born and raised in England. Meena knew that such a union would be intolerable to her family, not just because it had been arranged for her to marry somebody else but because of his nationality and different religion. The poor girl was in floods of tears. She had been like this for months. I was trying to comfort her when I heard something about marriage. It was not the arranged marriage but, I felt, a marriage between her and her soul mate. She looked straight at me. 'You are right,' she said. 'I married him last week.' Meena had gone off with her soul mate only the week before and had married at a register office, even while she was still living under her father's roof. She just knew that she had to be with him, that nothing could come between her and her soul mate. She knew that refusing to marry the other man would do no good. She would be forced to. If she ran away, her family would find her. This was the only action she could take to prevent this other marriage from taking place.

Meena was waiting to tell her family but she was very scared, for she knew that as soon as they heard the news she would be forced to leave home, and that she would never see her family ever again. Her family would never be able to cope with the shame their daughter had brought to them, and sure enough when she left they held a funeral of sorts for her.

Meena gave up a lot when she took this step and it cannot have been easy for her. But when forced to choose between true love and your family, I feel that you should always go where your heart is. The fact is, if your family really loved you, in a true and unconditional way, they would never put you into such a position, especially when you are in love already. Your family should only ever want you to be happy, and if you really know you have found happiness (as opposed to trying to spite your family!) go with it, rather than live a life of misery to please others.

You may be separated from your soul mate for years and years but that love, that feeling you had for the other person, won't die. However hard you try to fight your feelings, by moving in with another person, by marrying them, by shutting your soul mate out of your life for ever, not a day will pass without you thinking of them. Without your soul mate you will always find that there is something missing from your life, which is why, if you want to be happy in life, you must always be true to your soul.

Vanessa wrote me a letter asking for help. She said that she was at a crossroads in her life. She had been married for fifteen years and the last five years had been very difficult to cope with. Her marriage had been empty and unhappy. She confessed that early on in her marriage she had met a man with whom she had begun a deep love affair. It was love at first sight, and she felt that she had really connected with this man. But neither of them could stand the deceit of their affair and decided that it must end. They realized that they could never even see each other again. That was eleven years ago.

But as with true soul mates she could never get this man out of her mind, and recently she had begun having very vivid dreams about him. She wrote to him but never received a reply, which made her very unhappy. By the time I contacted her to offer her a reading she and her husband had split up. She was very sad and blamed herself for everything.

During the reading I felt very strongly that whilst her husband was a good man he was not her soul mate. I kept hearing the name Paul in my head, and with this name came the most intense feeling of true love. Vanessa confirmed that this was the man with whom she had the affair. She said that she had not seen him or heard from him since they had broken up.

But I felt very strongly in her reading that Paul was coming back into her life. He had never stopped loving her, it seemed, and when he had found out that she had split from her husband he felt that he could now come back to her. I told her that the first thing that he would say to her when they met up again was that she had not changed.

Vanessa, after years and years of denying her feelings, eventually realized that she had to follow her heart. She was lucky because Paul was free to do the same. And the first thing he said was indeed, 'You know, you haven't changed a bit!'

Many people in this situation give up hope. They do not believe that they will ever see their soul mate again, but just as the spirits encourage us to meet in the first place, they can bring them back to us again.

SIX

Happily Ever After?

Learning to Live With Your Soul Mate

Just because you have found your soul mate does not, I am afraid to say, mean that you will necessarily live happily ever after. Finding the perfect partner to share your life with is by no means the answer to all your problems. Don't imagine that just by meeting your soul mate your life will have a fairy-tale ending. Meeting your soul mate is, in fact, just the beginning. A relationship, after all, is not a fixed thing. A relationship is a journey that you and your soul mate make together. It is a journey that can be difficult and often tiring. There will be times when you may feel that you cannot keep up with the other. So to have a successful relationship with your soul mate you must help each other along this road and look out for one another.

The love you have with your soul mate is constantly evolving. As you live together you must grow together and make a world that you can share. Throughout your relationship there will be things that are sent to try you. You must learn together that you can overcome these problems so long as you are honest and true to each other. Happy endings don't come without a little work from both of you. You need to be there for each other every step of the way. As you live together you must grow together and make a world that you can share. The seed of love has been given to you both by a divine force and you must watch it grow and learn to nurture it before you can reap its benefits.

You may feel love for the person you live with but the love you have for your soul mate should always be free and without condition. Unconditional love is a very pure and very giving love as opposed to one that has limits and knows constraint. It is a love that allows us to be exactly who we are – not what the other person wants us to be. It is a love that encourages us to flourish and blossom as people. It does not see errors in the things we do and say, it takes us as we are. It is a love that is about mutual respect and understanding, compassion and caring, warmth and companionship. It is a lasting love.

This is a love that is not measured in expensive gifts and demonstrations. It is not about chocolates and flowers, fancy restaurants and foreign holidays. Unconditional love is a love that carries us through every single day of our lives. It is a love that enriches our lives and enables us to survive. However difficult times may get for us, if we know an unconditional love we will be stronger people, and thus find it easier to cope.

When we love a person in this way we love all of them. We take a person for who they are, warts and all, and continue to love them and to try to understand them. It is a love that asks for no reward, a love without condition.

The love you have for your soul mate should always be equal and mutual, but you will find that as your relationship progresses the roles you have will change, alter and adjust. There will be times when one of you is the stronger partner and the other is weaker. When one of you needs help, the other is there to give it. Soul mates are there to help each other through life, which is one of the reasons why we are given each other in the first place. Being sensitive to each other's needs and struggles can make life much easier for both of you.

One of the most common problems that people encounter in relationships with their soul mates is learning to cope with external pressures. Problems with money, children, family members, friends and work can all put a great deal of strain on even the most perfect relationships. External forces, outside of your relationship and outside of your control, can cause huge problems within it. Sometimes, because of the pressure we are under, we tend to turn on, or take it out on, the one person who is actually there to help us. We may say things to them we do not mean. We may cut them out of our lives, albeit temporarily. We may even think that they are responsible for how we feel. Always try to remember that your soul mate is always behind you. Even if you disagree on how to deal with a particular problem, that does not mean that you cannot try to work things out together. However bad things are getting between you, try to keep things in proportion. Your true soul mate would never deliberately do anything that would cause you pain, after all.

It is important in a relationship not to lose sight of each other. When things are bad, try to remind yourself what the real problem is. When we think of our soul mate not as our ally but as our enemy we have stopped communicating with those we love. Instead of giving them room to understand what is happening, we shut them out, preventing them from doing anything to help us or the situation. Try to get to the bottom of your problems together rather than blaming each other for what is going on.

Francesca and her husband David had been having problems for many years when she approached me. Things had got so bad for a time that she thought that their marriage might not be able to cope with the strain of what was going on. She tells her story here.

FRANCESCA

David and I met ten years ago. It really was a case of love at first sight. I knew he was my soul mate, and he was quick to tell me the feeling was mutual. Our romance was what you could call whirlwind. We met, dated, fell in love and within a year were married. At the start of our marriage neither of us had any money but it didn't bother us at all. It was never an issue. I was studying then and David had a new job in the recruitment industry. He wasn't particularly interested in it at the time, but it was a job and we needed the money.

We had said that we wouldn't have children for a couple of years until we were settled and more secure. We were happy as we were. But within months of our marriage I found I was pregnant. There was never any question that I wouldn't go through with the pregnancy. Our son may not have been planned but he was conceived with love. We made the best of it; I got a job and gave up my studies, David took on a second job doing deliveries. It wasn't easy but we needed a bigger flat and we knew it was going to take some time to save.

As my pregnancy continued I realized I couldn't go on working, and when Shane was born there was no question of me returning to work because I did not earn enough to have full-time childcare. David worked longer and longer hours to make ends meet. We rarely saw each other, and I cannot say that Shane was the easiest baby in the world to deal with, either.

We started having the odd fight, nothing serious, but it upset me because I remember thinking when I first met David that we would never ever argue. Now I know how naive this was. People who are in love do *row from time to time! Sometimes it can even be quite healthy.*

When Shane was two David lost his job. His firm relocated but we decided to stay where we were rather than move to an area we didn't know, following a job David never liked. It took him over a year to find another one. In the meantime I planned to go back to studying now that Shane was at pre-school, but found I couldn't because our income had been so cut. We sold our flat, which was sad, and spent the next three years moving from one rented place to another, never really feeling settled.

We fought more and more. David became increasingly withdrawn and uncommunicative, and I began to feel that our lives had turned into something terrible. What we now had together bore no resemblance to the life we planned originally. I felt that I had forced David to give up his dreams and the chance of a career because we needed money. And I also felt resentful that I had given up my studies to live this kind of life. Sometimes I thought if I left him he would be happy. I think that when you are under severe pressure you sometimes lose sight of what is important.

Things had got so bad at home that a friend suggested we went to marriage guidance. I could not bring myself to do this. I knew that if things had turned out differently for us in life, we would have had the happiest marriage on the planet. I also knew that David would never agree to it. But I had read an article about Rita Rogers in a magazine and thought if anyone could help us they would need to have pretty supernatural powers!

I wrote to her and asked for an appointment. She

read for me over the telephone and said that my grandmother, Lizzie, was coming to her. She correctly told me that I was the youngest of three, that I had two elder brothers and that my mother and father were divorced.

Rita said that she knew I was having many ups and downs in my marriage. She said that I shouldn't worry because Lizzie was going to look after me now.

Rita knew that my husband was called David. She told me, 'Don't leave him because you have had a bad time. It isn't your fault or his. He loves you so much. He really is your soul mate, you know.' Rita said that we had been very unlucky because of money and that we had both had to sacrifice a lot to be together. She said she knew that we had both come close to splitting up because of all this but she said that hope was coming. She knew about David's job and about selling our home.

Rita told me that our love is what had brought us through this time. She said that I would eventually have some luck with money, that I was to come into an inheritance that would help us out. She said that this would enable me to carry on with my training as a nurse, which astounded me because I had never told her what I had been studying for. She said that David would get a new job that would enable him to spend more time at home. It all sounded too good to be true and I wouldn't have believed any of the good bits had Rita not been so right about the rest. One of the last things she spoke to me about on the telephone was children. She said she knew that I had had a miscarriage a year before. I hadn't told David because I was worried about whether we could afford to have another baby. By the time I felt ready to talk to him it was too late. Rita said, 'Don't worry. You're going to have a lovely baby girl very soon.' I didn't know it at the time, but when I spoke to Rita I was pregnant. We now have a lovely baby girl and know now that we have a future together. We are still waiting on the inheritance, but Rita's been right about everything else!

Francesca and David were having serious problems, the kind of problems that might destroy anyone's marriage. But the problems were not between them, they were coming from outside of their partnership. Nevertheless, they were putting the couple under strain. Fortunately for them they always kept sight of the fact that they loved each other, and that is why their marriage survived.

Worries and problems do not disappear because we have found love, but what love can do is make things better. Never take for granted the very special healing properties that love can bring. Simply having someone around who cares for you can help take away the pain. Remember that your soul mate is there to help you through life. But they are not the answer to life's problems.

*

Another cause of strife between soul mates can be the presence of a third party. Three is always a crowd, and when an uninvited third party decides to disrupt the balance you have found together, one of you invariably ends up feeling left out in the cold.

The presence of a former lover or spouse can often be very difficult for soul mates to deal with – especially if it is your soul mate's ex, as opposed to your own. Such a person may end up undermining the love that you have found together. Problems occur here not because you cannot cope with the idea of your soul mate having a past, which is, after all, only natural, but because you are not allowed to get on with your relationship. This may be unintentional on the part of the ex, but in some cases it may be that the ex is determined to destroy your relationship.

I once read for a girl called Rachel. She was getting married in six months' time and was keen to know what the future held for her and her fiancé Ben. You see, although Rachel was mad about Ben, she had also been having second thoughts about the wedding.

When Ben and Rachel met, they fell in love instantly and decided within weeks that they wanted to marry. They knew that they were meant for each other, that they adored each other. At thirty-eight Ben was eleven years older than Rachel but the age gap did not bother them: they had plenty in common, and the difference they had in ages was bridged by their mutual love.

The problem they had was that Ben had been married before. His first wife Anna was causing trouble, meddling, always there. Ben had two children from this marriage and naturally was devoted to them. He had wanted to be close to them as they were growing up and so he and Anna lived very near each other in London. But Rachel was finding Anna's constant presence awkward. She was all for Ben being close to Anna for the sake of the children, but she found that Anna was difficult and often condescending.

In public, and especially in front of Ben, Anna was keen to play happily families. But in private she put Rachel down. Here Rachel explains how Anna nearly destroyed her future with Ben.

RACHEL

It was plain that Anna was unhappy about my relationship with Ben. There were constant digs, even attacks, nothing was good enough. If the kids came for the night she would call the next day to say one of them had an infection, blaming me, or that they had used bad language that they must have picked up around us. She would often make remarks about my age, wondering how I would cope with the children, never having had any of my own. At twenty-seven I didn't think that I was that young, and anyway I was brought up in a very large family, so I was used to looking after children.

The children had really liked me at first. Ben and

Anna had split up when the younger was only two, so I'm not sure that they remember much of a family life with them as a couple. I didn't think they would have too much of a problem coping with me; I wasn't trying to become their mother. But soon they began reacting strangely to me. Because of this Ben and I started fighting, which was awful. When I suggested that Anna might be trying to interfere in our lives, he said that she was a lot of things but she was a good mother. He didn't understand what I was talking about, so we argued all the more. What was supposed to be the happiest time of our lives was rapidly becoming the worst. At one stage it got so bad I thought about calling the whole thing off. That's when I went to Rita.

Rita told me that my grandfather, Tom, was in spirit and she told me, correctly, that he had died very young. She said he was my guardian angel and that he had sent me my soul mate. She told me about Ben, that he was my soul mate and said that we had a very deep bond between us, that we always got on well and that we knew what each other thought. She said it was a marriage made in heaven. I was heartened but surprised.

But Rita also knew that Ben had been married before and that he had two children, whom she named. She said that someone was trying to wreck our marriage, that they had the initial 'A' and then said that it was his first wife. But Rita told me not to worry. She said that our love was so strong that it would overcome all of this, and that in the end Anna would eventually give up. Rita confirmed what I had thought all along – that Anna was trying to turn the children against me because she could not bear the thought of Ben being happy with anyone else. She said that for the moment I had to be patient. She said that children could be impressionable but they were also quite wise and were able to pick up on things. In the end, she said, so long as Ben and I were happy together and always offered the children a warm and happy home, they would soon grow to love me. She said that Anna would retreat eventually.

Not long after our marriage Anna did give up her fight. A friend of Ben's had noticed how Anna was acting toward me and so he had a word with her. I think he made it pretty clear that he was unhappy with the situation. We are now very happy together and I am glad that in the end I didn't give up on Ben because of Anna.

Rachel's problem is not uncommon. I find it happens a lot with couples who are a bit older and, therefore, have more of a past, or might have been married before. Sometimes an ex-partner finds it very difficult to let go, even if that relationship has been doomed from the beginning. They sometimes find it more difficult in these situations because they cannot cope with the idea that true love and lasting happiness can be found with another person.

If this should happen to you try not to let it get to you too much, and whatever happens don't let it come between you and your soul mate. If you do, the third party is getting exactly what they wanted, and you are letting them win. If your love is strong enough, and if you are soul mates, it will overcome anything. And in time the third party will have to back down and retreat.

It is very important to have trust within your relationship. Trust allows us to live our lives when we are not by each other's sides. It is a confirmation of our love and faith in another person. It is a sign that we respect and honour another person's word.

Soul mates should always trust each other because they should believe that their love for each other is strong enough to overcome all things. However, sometimes when we love someone very deeply and with great intensity, this love may become too possessive. What is essentially a positive energy is in danger of being translated into a terribly negative force, one that can destroy the relationship.

Some of us are by nature jealous people. When we love someone very much we cannot imagine them sharing anything with anyone but us. Because of the love we feel sometimes we become possessive of our children, of our friends, and especially of our soul mate. The very idea of them talking to a member of the opposite sex, having friends other than ourselves, or being close to family members can cause great anguish. We start to become jealous of our soul mate being close to anyone other than ourselves.

I have over the years read for quite rational, intelligent people who are so jealous when it comes to their partner they are unable to cope when they are not with them. They tell me how they cannot bear it when their wife or husband even talks to another person on the telephone, how they hate it when they go away, how they assume that anyone who even speaks or looks at their soul mate must have some secret agenda.

Jealousy can be a good thing, as it comes essentially from feelings of love. But when it gets out of control it can destroy marriages and relationships as well as lives, as Sally Anne's story illustrates.

SALLY ANNE

My husband Ian committed suicide three years ago. I loved him very, very much and my life was destroyed when it happened. Afterwards I kept asking myself why. Why had a brilliant, caring, handsome man chosen to end his life in this awful way? There was no reasonable explanation for it. We had been married for eight wonderful years, had a five-year-old son and a lovely home. I certainly had everything that I had ever wanted or dreamt about. I thought that he had too, but when this happened all I could think was that he must have been terribly unhappy with his lot. Why else would he leave? For three years I believed this and just the thought of it made me sick with unhappiness.

Not only had I lost my husband, but my dream of how my life was. I thought it had been perfect but how could it have been if he wanted no part of it?

In 1998 I read From One World to Another *by Rita Rogers. I am not a spiritual person, but I was interested in the book because it contained a section in which a woman who had been in a similar situation to my own told her story. Her husband had also taken his life; she was my age. She described what had happened, how she had felt and how Rita had managed to help her make sense of his death. I'm not into mediums or anything like that but what she had said made such an impact on me that I was compelled to speak to her.*

I wrote to her asking for advice, thinking she would be far too busy to even answer my letter, but within weeks I had heard from her and an appointment was made. I did not want a reading as such, I just needed some help, but as soon as we spoke on the telephone she said my husband's name. I found this incredible as I had not mentioned it in the letter. She said that he was very sorry for what he had done, that it was a mistake and that one day he hoped that we, and she mentioned my son's name, could find it in our hearts to forgive him.

After my husband's suicide, our families and friends all tried to give me reasons why he had done it. Some said he was depressed, others said it was because he was unstable. I did not believe in any of this. I was his wife, I knew that even if he felt depressed he would never have done this to me or our child. He was not like that.

Rita, I suppose, confirmed the truth, something I had known deep inside but had kept from everyone who knew us. She told me that Ian had started drinking very heavily before he took his life. Because of this it had not turned out as he had expected. Rita said that he had only meant it to be a cry for help to get my attention because before he had died I had, if I am honest, not given him what he had needed.

Three years after our son was born I returned to work. I had always been quite ambitious and dedicated to my work. When I went back to my career I gave it everything I could to make up for lost time. I was working long hours, having to socialize with colleagues because of the nature of my job and I wasn't really around for my husband. When I was at home I was spending all the time I had being a mother. The only time we had together was when we were in bed at night and by then I was usually fast asleep.

By contrast, Ian was the type of man who had time for everyone. He was not ambitious although he liked to work. His main interest was family life. I think that he became resentful of my career, not because he wanted a life like mine, but because it was taking me away from him. He began to think I liked my job more than him. He was frustrated and so he began to drink.

Rita knew that he resented the time I spent away

from him, and that because he was drinking he began to resent me. The awful thing was that the more he behaved like this the longer I spent away from him. I think that when people get to his level they imagine all sorts of things. He would not admit to drinking, he did not understand that I did not want me or my son to be around when he was like this. One weekend it got too much and I took our son away. I only went to a friend's house, but it had all got too much. He had even accused me of having an affair – he had convinced himself that I was sleeping with my boss. He should have known this was absurd, but he wanted to believe it and he would not let it go. Two months later he took the overdose.

I believed Rita when she said that Ian did not mean to kill himself. Had he not been drinking then that dosage of pills he had taken would still have been a cry for help but it would not have been lethal. The problem with alcoholism is that you often don't even know that you are drinking. Rita said that Ian wanted to get my attention because he thought it would bring me back to him. The saddest thing of all is that I never even left. I believe Rita because everything she said was so true and so accurate that even a sceptic like myself could not doubt her. The irony is of course that I no longer work because I worry about our son not having enough love. I miss my husband so much. I cannot bear to think of the hurt he went through, the feelings of jealousy he experienced. The idea that he thought that I was capable of betraying him is so alien to me, which is why I probably did not take it seriously. Ian is the only man I have ever slept with. Even though he has now gone from life I would still like it to be that way.

If there are any lessons to be learnt from such a tragic story then it is that we must always try to channel our negative feelings in a positive direction. If you do feel jealous of a relationship you must work out in your soul whether you are a naturally jealous person and whether your concern is really justified. It may well be that you have got something totally out of proportion and have let yourself get carried away with your paranoia. You may have convinced yourself that there is something going on when in fact there isn't.

If you are not a naturally jealous person then ask yourself whether there is something going on in your life other than this which is making you feel this way. You could, for example, be suffering from low self-esteem or from a severe lack of confidence. You may be projecting your own insecurity into another form because you feel that you are undesirable or a failure.

When Sarah came to me for advice, it was because she had convinced herself that her husband was having an affair. I did not know this at the time of course, she told me later. I suppose she thought I could tell her the truth. In the end I did: he wasn't.

When she started to feel jealous there were a great

many changes going on in her life. She had just had a baby, which had meant that she had to give up work. She felt fat because she could not get her weight back to what it had been before the pregnancy, and she was also suffering from post-natal depression.

It was while she was at home looking after the baby she became convinced that her husband, Clive, was having this affair. He had started working extra shifts because they needed more money now that they had lost her income. Sarah was very resentful and felt trapped at home with the baby. Their sex life had suffered because he was tired from working and because the baby cried a lot at night, but Sarah became paranoid that it was because she was no longer physically desirable. Rather than talk to anyone about it, she convinced herself that he was betraying her, and to make matters worse she took it out on him without telling him what was really bothering her.

When I read for her I knew that he was not having an affair and that he adored her. I told her that she must stop looking for problems that did not exist and concentrate on what was really going on. A couple of months later Sarah wrote to me to say that she had taken my advice. They had taken some time off to be on their own without the baby, and had begun to get their lives back together.

Infidelity between soul mates is rare but it does happen. I say it is rare because true soul mates are monogamous by nature. Soul mates are not people who go out looking for someone else. When you experience love with a soul mate, when you have known that bond with another person, you stop searching for love elsewhere.

In my experience through my work, people who are serially unfaithful or promiscuous are people who are searching for something or, more accurately, someone. They feel that there is something missing from their lives, which is why they go from one person to the next. They are never satisfied, which is why they find it necessary to move from partner to partner.

However, all this said, we are only human. People do make mistakes and sometimes we find that other people tempt us. This is not unusual. After all, just because you have found your soul mate does not mean that you suddenly stop being attracted to other people, or them to you for that matter. As I have said before, when we are going through difficult times in our lives, we can lose sight of what is important. If we are feeling insecure, and are unable to communicate that insecurity to our soul mate for whatever reason, we look to other people to make us feel wanted and confident. It may be then that we feel attracted to another person.

If this does happen you should always be aware that the person you are attracted to does not offer anything more than you will find in your soul mate. The physical or even mental attraction you feel for the person is not anything in comparison to the love we feel for a soul mate.

More often than not it is only *after* you have strayed that you are left wondering, 'Was it worth it?' Was it worth the deceit, the inevitable pain and distress that your soul mate will suffer if or when you tell them the truth?

When you have really known love with a soul mate then the answer to this question will always be 'No, it wasn't worth it' – which is why people always refer to it as a 'mistake'. A relationship without love, however passionate it may seem at the time, is a relationship that will have no future, that has no depth, and that will leave you feeling empty. Even if you convince yourself that you are in love, that you feel things for this person, in time you will come to realize you were mistaken because you were not being true to your soul. By the time you have determined to go back to your soul mate, it maybe too late.

Infidelity can be a difficult thing for anyone to forgive. For it is not just the act itself that people find a betrayal but the dishonesty and deceit that go hand in hand with it. It can be very difficult to imagine that you could ever forgive your soul mate, but I find that given the right circumstances, you should try to give it another chance. True love should be able to survive even this.

Relationships do change as we grow together, but never assume that they change for the worse. It is only natural that as we spend more time with each other the love we have develops and becomes something different. The giddiness and sense of euphoria we felt when we were first with our soul mate subsides as we become more used to each other. The honeymoon period of our relationship ends and we find ourselves having to go back to the routine of our lives. But never imagine that the love you have for each other now is in any way less than what you have enjoyed before. It does, in fact, become much deeper and more profound.

Similarly, because of the pressures that come with life we may find that the freedom we enjoyed at the start of the relationship is no longer there. We are no longer able to sit up all night talking about nothing. Our plans for the future may have to be put on hold. The dreams we had for our life together may not be realized because of one thing or another.

Debbie telephoned me for a reading last year because she was worried about her marriage. She had been with her husband for nearly three years. Like any couple they had been having their ups and downs. I could tell this just by talking to her on the telephone, not through any psychic intuition but because her voice sounded strained and anxious. Her grandmother in spirit, a woman called Mary, told me she was married and that Patrick, her husband, was her soul mate. But when Debbie heard this she seemed surprised. 'Really?' she said. 'Are you sure?' 'Yes, absolutely,' I replied, and in order to confirm this I told her what Patrick did for a living and that he was working long hours because he wanted to buy a house of their own. Debbie then confessed to me that she had wanted a reading because she was not sure that Patrick was her soul mate and she thought she had made a terrible mistake by marrying him. She said she was so desperate she was thinking of leaving him.

I could not believe my ears. Her grandmother kept insisting that they were soul mates. Mary was telling me how wonderful this man was, that he was so kind, so considerate. She told me to tell Debbie that they would never break up.

Mary also told me that Debbie had just been to America. Debbie confirmed this and told me that she was thinking of going away again. The 'problem' in Debbie's marriage was not anything to do with her relationship with Patrick. It was to do with the fact that Debbie wanted to travel. When they had been first seeing each other they had talked a great deal about all the places they wanted to see but now Patrick was saying that he didn't want to go. Debbie took this to mean that he had gone back on his word, and that perhaps the man she married was not the man she first fell for.

Debbie had convinced herself that this meant that she and her husband no longer had anything in common because they wanted different things from life. But nothing could have been further from the truth. During the reading I picked up that Patrick was very worried about money. He was determined that he and Debbie should have a place of their own. And this meant making sacrifices for a couple of years, which explained her husband's reluctance to pack up and go abroad.

I assured Debbie that they would eventually find the

time and money to explore the world but for the moment she would have to be patient and not to worry. She had to learn that her husband still wanted what she did but for now they had other priorities. In the meantime I advised her to try to help Patrick. I told her that the man she married had not changed, just their circumstances. Patrick was not being selfish but was trying his best to do something for them and that she should love him for that. I told her that they would have plenty of time to travel the world later on because Mary told me that they would have a long life together.

It is always important in a relationship not to lose sight of why and how much you love the person you are with. Patrick and Debbie were destined to be together and were lucky to have found that love in the first place. We cannot always do the things we want to do in life. Sometimes we both have to make sacrifices. When you begin a life with someone, you have to realize that you are now part of a team. You cannot just go off and do what you want to do. You always have to take into consideration the wants and needs of your soul mate too. It may not be easy, but believe me it is worth it.

We may think when we begin a relationship with our soul mate that we have a lot in common and that we are by nature very similar characters, but living together can expose a multitude of differences. Even soul mates who are deeply and passionately in love at times find it difficult to live with their partner.

By recognizing our differences and by accepting

those differences and learning to communicate better we can enjoy more fulfilling relationships with our soul mates. Difference is not a bad thing, it can enrich our lives and make them more interesting.

Life is never a bed of roses. In times of pressure or difficulty we are all prone to being irritable, short-tempered or distant. Sometimes the pressure just gets too much and we say things we do not mean or behave in a way that is out of character. When this happens you must not immediately assume that your soul mate no longer loves you. Nor should you imagine that they have changed in any way, that they are no longer the gentle, kind person you thought you knew.

We all go through difficult times and sometimes we do not tell the person we are with and love because we are scared to, because we do not want to worry them, because we do not want to hurt them, because we love them. The problem here lies in communication. If your partner begins acting strangely for no reason try to find out why. Even if they turn you away keep trying.

The mistake many people make in this particular situation is that they begin to resent the way they have been cut out by their soul mate. Soul mates should never be afraid of telling each other things, but in some circumstances soul mates may keep things from each other because they do not want to cause alarm. Patience can play a very important role in a relationship. If someone cannot communicate with you about something, give him or her time and space until the moment is right.

You must learn to perceive that people see things from different angles in life: there is no black and white. Your soul mate may have come from a very different world to your own – they have grown up seeing things in very different ways, they have learnt different things, lived with other people. You must learn to allow them their experiences as well your own. Respect the choices they make, as they respect yours.

If you are going through a difficult patch with your soul mate keep reminding yourself of the following:

- Learn to give the relationship enough time and space to develop and improve.
- Remember why it is you fell in love with them in the first place.
- Learn to put things behind you and to forgive.
- Always respect your soul mate's differences and difference of opinion.
- Remember to listen.
- Understand the importance of keeping a promise.
- Remember that the problem you are having may be external.

SEVEN

Someone to Watch Over You

Learning to Live Without Your Soul Mate

Death is the only truth we have. Whatever happens to us in the course of our lives we know that one day we are all going to die. Yet despite the fact that death is inevitable, that we expect it, we tend to be very fearful of leaving this life behind.

One of the reasons why we are so scared of death is that we know so little about it. One's passing over is a journey into the unknown, a journey we will have to make alone. Even if we do believe that there is an afterlife of sorts we have no idea what it will be like, how we will feel when we die and what we will find when we get there.

I believe that our fear of dying stems largely from our inability to imagine a life away from this one. It is hard for people to imagine life continuing without them, to think of a world in which they no longer play a part. For most people it is not dying that frightens them, it is ceasing to exist.

People who have faith in religious or spiritual systems tend not to be so scared of death. This is because they have been taught to believe in the promise of an afterlife. Death for people with beliefs is not the end, but a continuation of a journey, whether that journey bring us back here, or takes us to another world.

But for people without any beliefs it is more difficult. For them death signifies the end; we become no more than dust and ashes. Death for people without beliefs equals nothingness.

Many people refuse to believe in the existence of an afterlife because it defies science. They cannot believe that it is possible to live on without their physical form. They think that because there is no scientific proof that there is an afterlife, it cannot exist.

But there are many things in this life which defy logic and reason. There are phenomena that cannot be explained. There are many unanswered questions. But just because we do not have all the answers does not necessarily mean that there is nothing after this.

In my work as a medium I have come across people who have never believed in anything. They are rational, logical, sceptical people who do not believe in an afterlife or spirits. And yet time and time again when people like this have lost someone very close to them, they have experiences that change their minds. Whether these experiences have come through readings with me, or have occurred in private, they have all spoken of the same phenomenon: an overwhelming feeling that the spirit of their loved one is still with them.

I always say that 'death' is not a word I like to use because I don't believe that there is such a thing. The experiences I have had through my work have convinced me that we *live on* after we 'die', albeit in another form. I always say that death is not the end but the passing from one world to another. Life does not stop at the grave, it continues.

If you believe that we have souls then you believe that life is eternal. Our souls exist separately from our physical form. The soul exists long before we are born into this world and continues to do so after we have left it. The soul has a life of its own, which is not reliant on the existence of the human body. Unlike the heart it is not an organ. The soul is invisible and intangible.

The self exists beyond the mortal form because the self is your soul. Who you are is not this body filled with blood and bones. Your body is merely a shell, a vehicle we use in this life. When we die our physical body becomes obsolete because it is no longer of any use to us. We enter a spiritual state, one that needs to be free from a body. We do not *become* spirits because we already are spirits. Our spirit has always been inside us, from the moment we were conceived. When we pass over it is still very much alive and is still growing.

Our bodies may give up but we take another form. Just because our physical form is now redundant that does not mean that our identity has died with it. What happens is that our spirits, our souls, our selves, move on.

The process is similar to the metamorphosis of the caterpillar into the butterfly. Your life on earth is symbolized by the life of the caterpillar. From larva, you grow into a caterpillar, you exist in that form and then one day you build a chrysalis. The chrysalis symbolizes our 'death'. The caterpillar does not know that when he emerges from the chrysalis he will become a butterfly, just as we do not know that when we die we will become spirits. Like the caterpillar in his chrysalis in death we change form. We discard the obsolete form of the caterpillar because it is a form we no longer need. And so we emerge as a butterfly. The caterpillar is not dead, he has simply changed his form. The butterfly, like the spirit emerging from the chrysalis, free and beautiful, is now able to go places it could never go before. The butterfly is the resurrected spirit of the caterpillar.

In the last chapter I discussed ways in which we can learn to live with our soul mates, here I want to talk about how we can learn to live without them – in other words, how to cope when your soul mate passes away before you do.

Grief is a very difficult thing to have to go through, particularly when it is our soul mate we have lost. Losing a child is without doubt one of the worst things that can happen to a parent because it seems so unnatural, but losing a soul mate is extremely hard as well. When we lose our soul mate we have lost the most important person in our lives, the person to whom we are closest. Not only do we often lose our lover, but also our best friend and our trusted companion.

Those first nights lying alone in a double bed can be terrifying. Waking up disorientated, reaching out for a body next to you to find the bed cold and empty is very difficult. There is no one there to talk to you last thing at night, or first thing in the morning. The prospect of facing life alone – especially if your soul mate has died relatively young – is very hard indeed.

When you lose your soul mate you realize just how much you took them for granted when they were here. When they go you are on your own, it seems you have no one to share anything with. Your weekends seem long and empty. Your mealtimes become bleak. Even a trip to the supermarket can make you aware of how lonely you really are. There is no one to touch, to hold, to be there for. There is no one to make you feel special. There is no one to love you.

When we love a person a great deal and they pass over it is very difficult for us to come to terms with the fact that they are 'gone'. Whether we are spiritual or not, in our own way we make them immortal. We create places for them, whether it is at the graveside or at home, we pore over letters, play music they liked, look at old photographs. We find ourselves talking out loud to them. There is absolutely nothing wrong with this, and in fact I would encourage it.

People who have never lost a close friend or lover may think that it is better not to mention them, to always change the subject when their name comes up in conversation, but what they don't understand is that most people find it important to talk about the soul mate they have lost. Talking about them keeps them alive for us.

You should never try to pretend someone didn't exist. They did, and they still do.

Grieving people tend to worry that they might forget bits and pieces about the person they have lost. They think that if they forget anything about them they will lose them for ever, which is why they hold on to their recollections of them. They cherish their memories of their loved one. But when someone we love passes away we should try when we are grieving not just to look at the past but at the future as well. For the person we have lost is in fact still very much with us and the love we had from them continues to grow, which why I say that love transcends death.

Just because a person whom we have known and loved in this life passes over into the spirit world that does not mean that the bond between us dies as well. Often it becomes stronger and more intense. In fact, I find that the bond between soul mates is so intense that I can usually tell within seconds whether the person I am reading for has lost their soul mate. As the spirit comes through and starts communicating with me I am always overwhelmed by an immense feeling of love.

When our soul mates pass away there should be nothing to be sad about, for they are still with us, they are happy, and they are living a richer, fuller life. In death, the only sadness should be for those who are left behind. When we grieve it is for ourselves, for the life we now have to live on our own. We should not mourn their passing but celebrate it. This is why I always say that the grave is for you and not for them. Funerals, graves, crematoriums – all these are for the living; they are symbols of the life we had down here. Do not look for the person who has passed away there, for they aren't there. We are conditioned to think that our loved one is in the grave. But all that is there is the shell they left behind when they entered the spirit world. Your loved one is always with you, around you, every day of your life.

Just because they are not physically with us doesn't matter because the love we shared and enjoyed with our soul mates was in essence so much more than the physical love we felt for them. The love we had for our soul mates was right from the beginning, a spiritual and emotional bond – an eternal love. Our soul mates are not in the ground, they are living on. They have not been taken from us. They are still with us, caring for us and watching over us.

When I talk about spirits watching over us, they are not actually 'over' us as such. The spirit world is not up there in the sky, suspended over the earth, like a heavenly canopy. It is all around us. The spirit world has no geographical location, it is not tangible. The spirit world, or the afterlife, is more like a higher state of consciousness than a place you can visit. I always say it is like being asleep and dreaming. This world is like your day, when you are awake, living your day-to-day life, your feet firmly on the ground. When we dream we move away from our physical bodies, into another consciousness, and we enter a different world. We can move around and experience things without our human form. This is what it is like to be in spirit too.

The spirit world is quite difficult to describe because we are so used to thinking in terms of matter and the spirit world is super-physical. It is not a three-dimensional world like the one we live in. It is neither concrete nor solid. And although the spirit world has no boundaries, it is structured into seven different worlds. These are known as astral planes. Each astral plane reflects a level of spiritual being. The first plane is the lowest, and is reserved for those who have committed crimes against other humans and shown no sign of remorse or regret. The second is for those who in life sinned and committed crimes but were sorry that they had done so later on. And so the structure continues until we reach the seventh plane, which is for those who have reached spiritual perfection. If someone has suffered a great deal in life, either physically or mentally, I find that they will go straight to this plane. Likewise children and babies go straight to the higher planes because they are pure and without sin. This structure is not fixed because the idea is that when we reach the spirit world we will grow spiritually until we eventually reach the seventh plane. Just as spirits are free to travel to this world they can also move freely between the planes. When we pass over we will be with our loved ones whatever the plane they are on. It is rather similar to being all at one large school but in different classes.

We are in spirit exactly what we were here on earth except that we have left our mortal form behind. We have a form that resembles how we looked here on earth but it is not fixed. When you meet your soul mate in the spirit world you will appear to them as you did when you were at the height of your love for each other. I mention this because it seems to be of great concern to some people. For instance, I once read for an old lady in her nineties. She had lost her husband during the First World War, she had never remarried, she was still very much in love with him and could not think of looking at another man. When she came to see me it was not because she wanted to contact him – she came because she wanted to know what she would look like when she reached the spirit world. She was worried that when she met him in the afterlife he would be a young man and she would be old and wrinkled! She was also scared that after all this time he might take one look at her and decide that she was far too old for him!

She should not have worried because there is no ageing process in the spirit world. In the afterlife, we all exist in our prime. It sounds like heaven to me! Those who have been disabled, in any way, down here, in spirit will be perfect. Similarly, anyone who has suffered from illness in this life will look and feel how they did before they became unwell.

I say that our soul mates who have passed over are always with us because while spirits like to spend time in their own world they are free to come to this world when they want to be with us. We have proof that they visit us through the messages they give us during readings. Often a spirit who has passed over will allude to some change that has happened in this world since their passing. It could be quite small, like a change in the decoration of a room in your house. They might tell me, for example, that they know that you have bought a new car or that you might be thinking of moving house. Sometimes their messages are more personal. They might know that you are pregnant, or that you have altered the style of your hair, or that you are having a row with someone in your family. When people first come to me for a reading they seem amazed that a spirit can actually be so specific. Someone who wants a reading may have come to me so that they can tell the spirit how much they have missed them since they have passed away, but here they are hearing about the extension on the house.

People seem very surprised by this at first but there is a logical explanation for it. The information that is being relayed to you may seem trivial but in fact it is very important because it is as though the spirit is trying to prove to you that they are still living and that they visit you regularly. They are giving us proof that there is such a thing as an afterlife.

Spirits come and go as they please. They come because they love us and because they are worried about us. They come to comfort us. They come because they miss us. They come because they hate to see us sad or lonely. They come at big events, like family get-togethers, weddings or the birth of a new child. They come when we want them to. Just because we cannot see, feel or hear spirits does not mean that they are not with us. They are always with us, watching over us like self-appointed guardian angels.

They will go to great lengths to communicate with the soul mate they have left behind. They do this because they are aware of the grief and unhappiness their passing has caused.

Spirits come to tell us they love us. They do not come to haunt us or scare us, they come to be with us because we need them. As I have said, when someone very close to us dies the grief we suffer can be extremely intense and overwhelming. Spirits may, in situations like these, come to us to let us know that they are OK and that they are happy. They worry about the soul mate they have left behind and so come to give them comfort.

I had known Ken Wright for years. When I first moved to the village where I live in Derbyshire, we went to our local pub one evening for a drink. I don't usually go out much because people tend to stare at me, to clear the room because they are afraid of me, or I get stuck in the corner having to tell them their life story. But the evening I met Ken we had gone out because we were new in the area and we wanted to see what the local was like. As I sat down at a table a very friendly-looking man came up to me and introduced himself. Ken was quite a direct sort of person. 'Are you one of those erm . . .

fortune tellers?' he asked nervously. 'I'm a medium,' I replied. 'Well, take a look at that then,' he said cheekily, pulling his hand from his pocket and opening his palm. 'Go on, tell me what my future is then.' 'I don't need to look at that to know what's going on in your life,' I said, pointing to his hand. 'I can read you just like that.' And I proceeded to tell him who he was and where he came from and what he did for a living. I mentioned that there was something wrong with one of the cars he drove at work. 'It's the break pads,' I said, which surprised even me, since I do not drive myself and know nothing about cars. 'My God,' he said, 'you're right, you are. I had them checked today.'

We had fun that night, Ken and I, and became firm friends from that point on. He used to visit the house quite regularly. He liked to come for a chat, and spent many hours with my partner Mo in the kitchen while I was doing my readings next door. But he would never come near my reading room. He said it gave him the spooks. He never really could get his head round what I did. He never had a reading after the night we first met, but we were friends nevertheless. In the winter months he would come and bring me bags of blue stalk mushrooms, which he had picked himself, because he knew they were one of my favourite delicacies.

Ken had been married to Jill for fifteen years. I only ever met her once, but I felt I knew her well enough because Ken would never stop talking about her. Those two really were soul mates. When Ken died suddenly last year after a short illness, I felt so dreadful for Jill I telephoned her the day after Ken had passed away to see how she was bearing up. While I was on the telephone I kept hearing Ken's voice in my 'inner' ear. This was strange because it usually takes a bit of time for a spirit to come through to me after they have passed over. But Ken's presence was overwhelming. As I was speaking to Jill I heard him ask me to tell Jill about his teeth. 'My teeth are missing,' he kept saying. He insisted that I tell Jill and that she must find them because he needed them for 'the long journey' he was about to make. Jill could not believe what I was saying. To tell you the truth, I was not really sure myself. But I knew I needed to pass the message on to Jill. Then Jill revealed to me that Ken had had a couple of false teeth at the front of his mouth. I had never known this.

Jill said that she had better telephone the hospital where Ken was still lying, to see if they were there. The doctor told her that they were missing. They searched his locker and the ward but they could not find them anywhere. She telephoned me that night in a real state. Ken came through again as clear as a bell. 'Look in the pot under the sink in the bathroom,' he said to me. Jill went to the bathroom. 'They're here!' she said, amazed. Do you know, Jill had never known where Ken put these teeth in all the year's they had been married!

About ten days after this incident I was interviewed on a radio programme on our local station, Chesterfield 106. I was in the middle of a live phone-in when a healer, whom I had never met, rang the station and asked to talk to me. There were quite a few calls coming through the switchboard at the time but this healer insisted that it was urgent. I agreed to take the call. 'Rita Rogers?' he said when we were finally connected, 'I have a spirit here called Ken Wright. He keeps telling me I must get hold of you and that it's urgent.' For the life of me I didn't know what he was talking about, for in all the years I had known him I had never known Ken's surname. If I did it had slipped my mind; anyone who knows me well will tell you that I'm a great one for faces but terrible at remembering people's names. The healer went on, 'Mrs Rogers, this Ken here is saying that he must speak to Jill, it's very important. He says he needs to tell her how much he loves her.' It was then I realized it was Ken.

That night I was sitting at home about to dial Jill's number when I got a call from a colleague of hers. She asked me to call Jill and talk to her because she was in a very bad way, she was missing Ken a lot and there were things on her mind that were troubling her. I put down the telephone and rang her immediately. Jill tells the story from here on in her own words.

JILL

I was at home listening to the radio programme. Rita Rogers was on. I did not really know Rita well. I had never been for a reading with her, but she was a great friend of my husband's. I listened in that day because

Ken had always been such an admirer of Rita's work. The show was going on as planned, when suddenly I heard my husband's name mentioned. 'Ken, Ken Wright,' this healer was saying. He was telling Rita to tell me that Ken needed to speak to me. I could not believe what I was hearing.

Ken had not long passed away. He had suffered an illness of the bowel. It had disintegrated, because blood was not getting there and there had been nothing that anyone could do to save him. He was only fifty. I was missing him so much and found there were things I could not cope with. He went so quickly and there were a lot of things I would have liked to have sorted out, to have been able to say to him, before he went.

I had always believed in an afterlife but I could not really believe that this was happening. It was amazing. First Rita had told me about Ken's teeth but she had also helped me find a very important document soon after Ken's death. When he passed away it was so sudden that I was unprepared for it and I did not know where he kept a lot of his papers. I turned the house upside down searching for this document but had no joy. 'Ken's saying it's on the top floor of the house,' Rita kept saying. I knew it wasn't. I had been into my bedroom, which was on the top floor, and searched it, but I hadn't found it. When I told Rita this she said, 'Not your bedroom, Jill. Ken says the top floor of the house.' And then I understood he meant the attic. I put down the telephone and rushed up to the attic and there it was.

I could not believe that Ken had gone to so much trouble to help me sort things out in the days after his death. First the teeth, then the document and now contacting me through the radio show because he knew I was down. It was quite amazing.

I feel good knowing that Ken is really with me. Because of what happened I now understand that he is with me. Too many things tell me he is. I know when he is with me because he blows gently on my face. We were together for fifteen years and I know that he was my soul mate. As I say now, you never know what you've got until it goes away.

Jill and Ken were very lucky to have had the love they did. Ken is a wonderful spirit. I can feel him quite often and when he does come through I always feel this tremendous warmth and love for Jill. In January this year, I was in my sitting room with my hairdresser chatting away when the doorbell rang. 'That'll be Ken with my blue stalks,' I said. My hairdresser went to the door and answered it. I could have sworn for an instant that it was Ken standing there with a bag in his hand but actually it was the landlord of the local pub. 'Mrs Rogers, I thought you might like these,' he said handing over the bag. I opened it. It was full of blue stalk mushrooms. I don't know why I said it was Ken when the doorbell went.

Habit I suppose, or maybe, just maybe, Ken had wanted me to know that he wouldn't forget my blue stalks.

You don't have to visit a medium to know that your soul mate visits you. Jill said, in her story, that she knew when Ken came to her because he blew gently on her face. At certain times, spirits like us to know that they are there for us. It is rare that they will show themselves directly to us but they have other little ways of letting us know that they are around. It is not unusual, for example, to experience a sensation of sudden warmth, love and happiness, for no apparent reason. You may be feeling quite down when this happens, or worried, so you cannot really explain why you suddenly feel this tremendous surge of emotion. It is as though someone has lifted your heart. And just as suddenly as it comes, it goes. What is happening here is that the spirit is letting you know that they are with you, that they love you and that they are there for you even though you cannot see or hear them.

The reason why we are able to experience such things when we lose our soul mates is because the love that you have in this life tends to make this spiritual link much stronger. In my experience your spiritual bond is stronger the more in love you have been.

Spirits like to give us signs that they are still around us. They may start moving things around the house, small objects for example, and they are quite keen on messing around with the electrics. Many people have told me how their spirits like to play with radio or television sets, that they turn the lights on and off, or how they like to change the temperature on the central heating system. An elderly gentleman I read for says that the spirit of his wife Aileen likes to make the telephone ring from time to time, as if to let him know that she is there. He says that he knows it is her because every time this happens he feels a warm, pulsating feeling in his chest.

A lot of people have said they sense the smell of their soul mate long after they have passed over. They may be away from the home, at the office, or somewhere where there would be no trace of their soul mate's scent, yet it just wafts over them. One man told me how he was varnishing the floor one day when all at once he could smell his wife's Chanel No 5, which is not a smell one would normally confuse with wood varnish. There have been times when I have been sitting in my reading room on my own when my eyes have begun to water from the heady scents of aftershave or perfume.

Spirits are also very attracted to music. Playing a particular record that had meaning for your soul mate can draw them to you. Often people have said that they have felt their soul mate in the room when a certain piece of music was being played. They may not even be thinking of their soul mate at the time when this occurs. The piece may not even be very sentimental, but they come because they want to be with us at that moment. This happened to me when my late husband Dennis's father died. Dennis's father had always been a great fan of music. One afternoon after he died we put a couple of his old 78s on the record player and I was, at once, overwhelmed by his presence.

Some spirits like to show themselves to us through animals and insects. It is important to realize that in these cases the animal who comes to you is not your soul mate metamorphosed or reincarnated. What happens is that spirits use birds and small animals, and temporarily take possession of them. I know people, for example, who have hated cats and yet when their soul mate has passed over have described how they spent days and days being followed around by some stray and have felt compelled to give it affection. Sceptics would argue, of course, that these people are imagining things, and that they have shown warmth to an animal they have not liked before because they are lonely or perhaps, bored. I am afraid I don't agree with this argument; for I have witnessed too many strange cases of possession in my lifetime to pass this subject off lightly.

I once read for a lovely lady from America who had lost her teenage daughter. I was reading for this woman on the telephone one afternoon when a queen bee flew through my reading-room window and rested on my knee. Normally, I would have been scared that the bee would have stung me, and I would have flinched away from it. But that day something told me not to be scared. A voice in my 'inner ear' told me that it wouldn't sting me. The queen bee seemed happy sitting there on my knee so I just carried on with reading. At the end of the conversation I asked the lady if she knew whether there was any significance to this. She was astounded, for 'Queen Bee' had been her daughter's nickname. When I put the telephone down the bee flew out of the window.

Spirits seem very fond of butterflies too. This seems appropriate because in many cultures the butterfly is a symbol of resurrection. Another lady I knew said that a blue butterfly spent a whole afternoon resting on her hand the day of her husband's funeral. Blue was always his favourite colour and she took it as a sign that he was there and living on.

When these animals or insects do come to us they are always very peaceful and friendly. In fact, usually they are much tamer than they would normally be in nature.

Jackie lived in a top-floor flat of a tower block in England. One day she opened her window and there was a large, bronze-coloured pigeon sitting on her sill. Jackie could not believe it for they must have been over 145 feet up. He stared at her and didn't move. Jackie put her hand out as if to touch him but the bird did not fly away. Instead it inched nearer to her outstretched hand and then let her stroke it. It seemed so happy and affectionate that Jackie leaned over and kissed the bird. It stayed there for a while and then flew off. The bird returned the next day and spent hours sitting on her still. She did not feed it but the bird kept coming back. In the end Jackie became convinced that the bird was the spirit of her late husband. The bird's visits started three days after he had passed away and continued for about a week.

Often these possessions do not carry on for too long. Spirits only really like to show us they are near us when they know that the one they have left behind is grieving. They come for a while to let us know they love us and then when we are happy they go away.

For some people the experience they have when their soul mate visits them can be much stronger and more intense than the ones I have talked about so far. It is very unusual but there are instances when a spirit may try to communicate with you by actually speaking to you.

I once read over the telephone for a woman in Wales called Rosemary. She and her husband had been soul mates and had been madly in love. She was devastated when he died. When I read for her, her husband came through immediately. His voice was very clear and strong. He told me that he visited her and watched over her, giving me details of things that had happened since he died. He told me to tell her that she had a hole in her roof, for example. He went on to tell her through me how much he loved her and that he wanted her to know that he would never stop loving her even though he had passed away. At that moment Rosemary, overcome with emotion replied, 'God I feel so close to you now.' And then, down the receiver, as clear as glass, a man's voice said, 'I love you.' We both heard him. Rosemary said it was definitely her husband, she could tell by his distinctive voice. She was so moved she fell silent. It was a very beautiful moment.

As I have said earlier it is very rare for a spirit to

actually show him- or herself to us directly. Spirits can appear to us but to do so they need to use a medium through which they can transfigurate. Transfiguration is sometimes referred to as materialization and it is the process by which a spirit is able to show itself to those on the earth plane. It is a very rare psychic phenomenon and it takes a great deal of skill and patience on the part of the medium.

However, it is possible to see the spirits of our soul mates, in dreams. I am not talking here about the normal dreams we might have at night where our brain shows us images of things and people we have been thinking about that day. But dreams that are so vivid and lifelike that when we wake from them we are convinced that they must have been real in some way. What I am describing here is a phenomenon known as astral planing. We may feel that when we wake from such an experience we have actually been with our soul mate. That they have come to us in a dream and that we have spent hours talking to them and being with them in some other world. And in a sense we have.

Nikki loved her husband Lee very much. So much so she could not bear to part from him even when Lee went to work. Their doctor had just told Nikki and Lee that they were expecting their first child when he was killed in a road accident. The shock nearly made her miscarry.

Nikki was very strong during her pregnancy, she felt she had to carry on for the baby. After the birth, however her emotions caught up with her. When she saw her child for the first time, she burst into floods of tears, for although she was overjoyed to see the baby she also realized that she was on her own. Her husband should have been there for this special moment but he had gone. It was then that she realized he was never coming back. She kept thinking to herself, 'If only he could see his child once.' But she knew it was impossible. Or so she thought.

That night she went to sleep and had an out of body experience. She felt Lee come to her, take her hand and lead her to the side of the crib where their baby lay sleeping. She said that it seemed like she was there for hours. They did not speak but he had his arm round her. She didn't tell many people about what had happened that night, because she thought that they would dismiss it as just a dream, but she knows that it was much, much more than that.

Astral planing is not uncommon. However, in all my years as a medium I have never come across a story as strange and as beautiful as Susie's. I got a letter last year from this woman in Australia, whose husband had just died, and he was very young. Susie found it very difficult to cope at first, she struggled to get by without him. Months later Susie had a very 'lucid' dream, as she put it, in which she met her husband. He showed her where he was in spirit. She said, 'It was a place like here, but more perfect.' She told me that while they were together they made love spiritually. 'It was the most fantastic feeling,' she said. 'It was as if we had merged.' Susie said that when she woke up from the dream she knew she had to let him go because her grief was making it difficult for him to leave her. She said that the dream had been so real that it had given her the strength to carry on with her life at last.

When I read for Susie her mother came through to me very clearly. She was saying to Susie that she had a surprise for her, she was bringing her husband to her and that he was very handsome. He was carrying a yellow rose, she was telling me. Susie's mother told me that he had died tragically in an accident in his twenties, that there had been a vehicle involved and that one day he just didn't come back from work. She said that Susie had been pregnant with her second daughter at the time and that her husband was pleased that she had named the child Leslie after him.

He then came through and told me that it had taken him a long time to ascend because he didn't understand that he was 'gone'. He knew that Susie had been in hospital when he passed away because she was so upset, but he was happy that she was OK now. He told me how she had remarried, what her husband's name was and how he was grateful that he was taking care of his family now. He then told me that he wanted her to know that she was not dreaming that night. He had bent the rules and had taken her into the spirit world. He wanted to keep her there but he knew he had to bring her back for the girls. But he knew that the trip would be wonderful and that it would help her get on with the rest of her life.

At the end of the reading he kept telling Susie, through me, how much he loved her, and I could not help feeling how lucky she was to have known such a love.

Astral planing is rare in that I find that it only usually occurs between people who have had a strong bond and love for each other, such as soul mates, or when parents have lost their children. It is not a frightening experience. The spirits come to you to be with you and give what you need. They do this because they love you and then they go.

But sometimes our soul mate can end up spending more time with us than they should. I once read for a woman called Norma. She and her husband had been very much in love and had been together for over forty years. They did everything together. When he died she felt very sad, but she counted her blessings, and was thankful that they had had each other for so long. She tried to get on with her life as best she could.

Norma was not the type of woman who made things up. But one day not long after he had passed away she was in her kitchen doing the washing up when she felt her husband's hands in the water, on top of hers. She pulled her hands out, fearful that she might be imagining something. But when she immersed them in the hot, soapy water a second time, she felt them there again. They were holding on to hers. There was no doubt in her mind that this was actually happening.

But it did not stop there. More and more strange things began to happen to Norma. Often when she was alone she would feel the spirit of her husband hold her hand. As a couple they had enjoyed watching snooker on the television but Norma did not like to watch it on her own. One night when she was sitting there on her own and tuned into some movie the television swapped stations – to the snooker.

Over the following months these meetings became more intense and strange. She would feel the side of the bed go down when she got into it at night as though he were getting in with her. It was as though he would not let go of her, he was living as though he was still alive, as though nothing had changed. When he grasped her hands in the sink that day it was as though he wanted to be with her, as though he were pulling her into the spirit world. But no matter how much a spirit loves us they cannot take us there until the time is right.

These encounters were beginning to drain Norma. When she came to see me she was distraught. She stayed for two days and during this time the spirit was constantly with her. I told him that he must leave and that he could visit but that he should not stay with her because it was beginning to make her ill. Norma had also to let him go in her heart. It was a hard choice for Norma to make because she did love him so, but it was one she had to make. Eventually the spirit ascended. Norma misses him dreadfully and can't wait to be united with him in the spirit world, but for now she knows she must get on with the rest of her life here.

*

The pain of losing someone we really love can often be too much to bear. Many people feel that once their soul mate has gone they cannot continue living. If they cannot be here with their one true love they would prefer not to live at all. Those who believe in an afterlife long to be reunited with their soul mate in spirit. Those who feel that there is nothing after this would gladly trade life for nothingness, such is their despair.

When our soul mate is taken from us it is as though part of our spirit is taken away too. If the bond of love has been especially strong people often feel as though they are now only half a person. Many people tell me that they wish they could have gone too. They feel that there isn't anything left for them down here any more. Many people ask me if I could ask their soul mate to fetch them. Some ask me how long they have left down here, because they are not sure they can take it any more. Some people seriously consider taking their own lives.

If your soul mate could come for you they would, because there is nothing that would upset them more than knowing you were suffering in this way. However, your destiny is not in their hands. When your soul mate reaches the spirit world they will know how long you have left on this plane. They know also that it is not up to them to change your destiny. They know you must live out your life as best you can. They may try to make things easier for you, either by visiting you or by sending you a companion or karmic soul mate (See Chapter

Eight), but usually they cannot fetch you before your time. But when you do pass over, they will be there to collect you.

You should not take it upon yourself to interfere with your own destiny either. Try to remember that you are here for a reason, whether it is for your children, your friends or to do something important. However deep your despair is, however lonely you are, be patient. You must remember that when you do pass over you and your soul mate will have eternity together – which should be enough time!

I do believe, however, that some people can die of a broken heart. My own grandmother, not my Romany one but my mother's mother, died of a broken heart. She had had eight children and lost three to tuberculosis. She grieved so much for her little ones she just could not carry on after that.

Soul mates often die of broken hearts. They are like lovebirds, unable to carry on without their mate. You hear of these cases so often, especially with elderly couples. When some old people lose their soul mate, they lose their reason to live. They may not have anyone else in their lives, so they begin to shut down. Their reason and will to live fades away, making them sick. It is like when you cannot stop crying. You cry so much, you eventually begin to hurt. You get a pain in your chest near your heart, and you begin to feel the effects of your emotions physically. In cases such as these, when a person's whole purpose for life has gone and their time is nearly due anyway, I do think that spirits allow them to follow their love into the afterlife.

For those who have not found love in this world for whatever reason they are guaranteed to find it in the next. For we all have a soul mate with whom we are destined to spend eternity. In my work of reuniting parents with the spirits of their children who have passed over I have encountered many instances of this. Children who have passed away do grow up in spirit, reaching the age of twenty-one, and when they come through to their parents they very often bring with them a soul mate they have met in the spirit world. It is as though they are bringing them home to meet their parents. It does make me happy when this happens, because I think that so many parents who mourn the loss of their child's life here think that it's sad that their child will never experience the feeling of being in love. Knowing that they have this chance in the afterlife, and knowing that their child is not alone either, makes it easier for such parents to cope with their child's death.

People who have suffered a great deal in this life through disability or illness and who because of that have not been able to find a soul mate down here, should also know that as soon as they reach the spirit world they will find a soul mate there. It will be someone they could have met down here, or even did meet down here, but perhaps were unable to be with because of their condition.

We are all perfect in spirit, so however much you have suffered through illness or disability in this life, in the spirit world you will look just as you *should* have looked down here had you not been unwell. I know this because I have read and transfigurated the spirits of a great many people who have suffered in this life. Their parents, soul mates and families have said that when they have come through in a transfiguration that they are overwhelmed by how beautiful they really are. I would also like to point out that anyone who has suffered through illness or disability in this life is *not* being punished for something that they have done in a former one. Such a suggestion is absurd. Nature and fate can sometimes be cruel, but whatever imperfections we have to suffer in this life will be corrected in spirit.

For people who have been too ill or too young to find love here, you should know that when you reach the spirit world you will not have to wait long to find love. Your soul mate will be there waiting for you and it will be very clear, even instantly, that they are for you. Whatever happens to you never give up hope because love comes to us all eventually.

Two years ago I read for a very special woman called Sally, who works at a hospital in London. This is her story.

SALLY

I wrote to Rita in 1997 because I needed some guidance. I work as a relaxation therapist and aromather-

apist in the leukaemia unit of my local hospital. The unit I work in actually specializes in bone marrow transplants. The problem this unit faces is that there are very few donors, so the future of the people I work with is always in the balance. Even if the patients do get the transplants they need, the survival rate is sadly not high.

In my work you get very close to people. It is hard not to be involved. And being around so much death was becoming confusing. I needed some guidance and also some answers, so I booked a telephone reading.

In the months before I spoke to Rita I had been working with two people who I had become extremely fond of. They were called David and Susan. Both David and Susan were in the acute phase of leukaemia when I met them. They both desperately needed a donor but were finding it difficult to find a match. They were both in their early twenties and although they were aware of each other at this stage they had yet to become friends. Yet David and Susan had a lot in common, not just their illness or their age. Both were Jewish, and for Susan this was very important. You see, getting bone marrow donors to come forward can be difficult and finding matches can be even harder. This is because there is not enough information given about transplants and certain religious groups think that it goes against their doctrine. For people from ethnic backgrounds the situation is more difficult because not enough people from those communities are aware of the need for bone marrow donors. Susan had even set up an organization that promoted donor awareness in the Jewish community.

I work as a catalyst; I try to bring people together. It is like being the third point in a triangle. In a hospital scenario it can be helpful to meet someone who is in a similar situation to yourself. I thought that it would be good for David and Susan to meet, and when they did, they got on really well.

In the end they both found donors, Susan finding hers from her organization. But, sadly, neither David's nor Susan's transplants worked. They both died within weeks of each other.

When I spoke to Rita I knew she must be genuine because the first spirit who came through was a little girl who had been in my unit. Rita asked if I knew a Katie. She said that she was very young and that she was telling her that she had made a bracelet for me. This was true – she had, the week before she died. I found this very reassuring as I knew now that there must be life after death, but it also scared me. I am a spiritual person but however much we want to believe in something I think that we all have a bit of scepticism in us.

Rita then told me she had a David with her. I knew who she meant at once. She told me he had died of leukaemia and that he had come to tell me he was happy. She said, 'He's come with Susan. And he's telling me that they are soul mates.' I cannot tell you how this made me feel. This coincidence, the fact that they were now together and were coming to me as a couple, was quite amazing. I had not discussed either David or Susan with Rita until that point in our conversation. I knew that they had been friends at the end, but I had not imagined that there was anything more. It was such a wonderful thing, and this experience has made what I do easier.

David and Susan came to Sally to show her that there was meaning in what she did. They knew that she was confused. I know from all the very brave doctors, nurses and carers I meet that it isn't easy being around so much sickness and death, especially if you have doubts about the existence of life after death in the first place. Sally did a very important thing for this couple without even realizing it the time. She was responsible for introducing David and Susan. As soul mates they would have found each other in the spirit world anyway, had they not met here. But thanks to Sally they were able to enjoy each other at the end of a very difficult life. It was fate that they were in that hospital at the same time, and fate that guided Susan to introduce them. And I am sure that when they did pass over, they were happier, knowing that they had found each other, and that it would not be long before they were reunited for ever.

EIGHT

Other Souls

SAME-SEX SOUL MATES

Our souls exist as entities long before we are born, long before we take on our physical form. Souls have no sex, no nationality, no colour and no creed. It is only when we are born into this world that we become those things. In spirit they have no relevance because none of those things are what we are in essence; they are only mantles that we take on in this life.

Soul mates are paired because they are spiritually compatible, not because of their future sex. When you were given your soul mate it was because they were right for you, not because they were to be the 'opposite' of your sex. Therefore, you can have a soul mate that is the same sex as yourself, just as you might have a soul mate who is from another country, from another religious background, from another social class or who is a different colour from you.

A same-sex soul mate may not necessarily become your lover. However, spirits are not prejudiced; they do not judge any one of us because of colour, creed, age, sex, sexuality or position. To them such things are irrelevant because when we pass into the spirit world all we take is our soul, because that is what is of value, nothing else. What we are on the outside is of no importance: it is what is *in* us that matters.

We have different sexes here on earth because it is important for us to reproduce in order to create life. But in the spirit world there is no reproduction. Before our birth the soul is not so much sexless but of both sexes, Oriental philosophy talks of this in terms of yin and yang. It is only after our conception that our sex becomes one or the other.

Sadly, there are a great many people in the world, even people of education and intelligence, who do not see it this way. They believe that all soul mates should be male and female. They are misguided.

I have dealt with many parents over the years who are sadly prejudiced about their child's sexuality, and find it difficult to comprehend that such a state of affairs was meant to be. 'Its unnatural! If only she could meet a nice man,' they say. Or, 'If Brian were to fall in love truly, I mean with a woman, I would feel happier for him. ' Or, 'He won't be happy being gay because he'll never find true and lasting love that way.' True, there aren't such things as gay soul mates. But only just as in the same way there aren't such things as heterosexual soul mates. Or just as there aren't such things as Asian or African-American soul mates for that matter. Soul mates are just soul mates. They aren't any kind of other mate, by definition.

I feel very sorry for people who are in situations like these. Love is love: it knows no boundaries, no prejudices or conditions. As I have said throughout this book, you love *people*, as they really are deep down, deep within. Loving someone of the same sex as you is no different, certainly no less, than loving someone who is of the opposite sex.

As I said in the last chapter, always go where your heart is. If your family and friends cannot accept you for who you are, for what you want and for who you want to be with, then they are not offering you real love. You must be true to yourself and not let others mould you into what and who they want you to be.

Three people I used to read for come to mind. A mother and father, who would come to the reading together, and their daughter, who was dragged along and whom I would read for separately. When the parents came to me they would always ask the same questions: 'When is Lisa going to find her man?' 'When will Lisa get married?' 'How many children will Lisa have? We do so want her to be happy.' And so it went on.

Lisa was only twenty-seven but we both knew when she came for a reading that Lisa was never going to get married and that Lisa was not going to have children. Lisa would be happy, and she would find her soul mate eventually, but at the time she came to me she was a very sad and confused individual. The fact was, Lisa was gay. She had known this most of her adult life but whilst she was happy with her sexuality she knew her parents would not be. So for years Lisa had been living a double life, bringing boys and men back to meet her parents, pretending that she was 'normal'.

It was her grandmother, who had passed away some years before, who told me that Lisa was a lesbian. It came through to me in her reading, and her parents'. But whilst Lisa and I could talk openly about her sexuality and how it affected her life, it was not something I discussed with her parents. Her grandmother told me to wait, that the time was not right. She felt that Lisa should go away to America for a while and experience a life of being true to herself. When she had done that, and when she felt comfortable and strong enough, she should come back and tell her parents the truth. Lisa had in fact already made plans to do this, and she left for the States some months later.

I never lied to her parents. Her mother asked me during one of our last readings whether Lisa would meet her match out there. 'Yes,' I replied because I strongly sensed that America was indeed where Lisa would find her soul mate.

I do not believe that anyone should be forced to live a double life or a lie. But in Lisa's case I thought that she needed time to become her own person and feel confident again before she approached the subject with her parents. Her parents' constant talk of husbands, weddings and grandchildren had worn her down; she was being made to feel as though she was letting everyone down, which is not a good state of affairs to be in. Lisa and I hoped that the break would offer all of them a chance to appreciate what is important in life. For Lisa that meant becoming her own person; for her parents, an understanding of how much they missed and loved their daughter, whoever she chose to be.

We all want the best for our loved ones, particularly our children, but often what is best for us is not best for them. However difficult things are for us to understand we must learn to accept them for who they are. Surely it is better for your daughter to find fulfilment and true love and happiness with a member of their own sex than to live in an empty, loveless marriage until the day that they die? We always say we want what is best for our loved ones because we love them, but what is best for anyone is without doubt love, happiness and truth.

What I would say to a parent who is finding it difficult to come to terms with their child's sexuality is to try to understand what it is like for them. To feel outcast from your own family at such a time, a time when you yourself are trying to understand who you really are, is very hard. We all need our families, but I feel in the case of homosexual couples they need them all the more, for often it is the only family they will ever have.

Times and attitudes have changed. People should no longer feel that they are doing wrong by following their heart. Your soul mate is your soul mate because you have a spiritual bond. You love them, and they love you, for your soul. Not your colour, creed, sex or political beliefs.

Sometimes it takes us a little longer to realize who

we are than it did for Lisa. Steve was married to Helen for eight years and they had two children. He thought he was gay but at the time he could not come out because he felt it would not have gone down well with either his family or his friends. He tells his story here in his own words.

STEVE

When I met Helen I really loved her: she was wonderful, beautiful and kind. I knew that she was going to be a lovely wife and a good mother. But the fact was, as much as I adored her and she me, we were not soul mates.

When I met Mark at the bookstore where I worked there was this instant bond and rapport that I had never known with my wife, however much I tried and tried. I did not think suddenly, 'I am gay.' It wasn't a physical thing but purely emotional. There was just something about this man, something within him. His sex was not what I initially thought about. When I visited Rita about trying to contact my dead father, although I suppose now that was not really the reason I approached her, she told me Mark's name. She said she thought I had found my soul mate. She didn't seem flustered by it, and I remember being very calm.

But she did say, 'You must go now and tell Helen so she can find her soul mate, because she will soon, and then she won't be sad.' Helen wasn't actually so sad when I told her, a bit surprised perhaps, but she

> *didn't judge me. But she was worried about our children; not because I was with a man now, they were too young to understand that, but because she thought it was important that we stayed friends. We have, and Helen has her 'own boyfriend' as she says, too. These days she is funny about it all and likes to tease me. She says she always knew we were not soul mates and she is happy that I have found mine and she hers.'*

Finding out who you are sexually is very much caught up with finding out who you are spiritually: it is about discovering yourself.

Beth, who lives in New York, had been seeing a girl called Jo for about eight months. Jo was not Beth's first girlfriend. Beth had been seeing both men and women for many years, but Jo had never been involved with a woman before. They met in the summer and got on very well. Jo stayed with Beth over those months and the two quickly fell in love. They soon felt very strongly for each other – it was a very intense beginning. But then Jo had to leave for England. She said she had to visit her family, who were living there, and to pick up some of her things.

Beth did not think anything of it until she received a letter one morning from Jo. It was very nasty and cruel. She said she never wanted to see Beth again, that she could no longer be friends with her and that she blamed her for turning her into something that she was not. 'I wish you had never touched me, ' she wrote. 'I want to forget this ever happened. I want to be with a man.' The letter horrified Beth and hurt her. She felt that at no time during their relationship had she forced Jo to become gay. 'It was never like that,' she said when she telephoned me for a reading. 'It was not a "gay" thing, we were just two people who met and got on straight away. We clicked and we were very happy, or so I thought. I thought that in Jo I had found my soul mate, and I can honestly say that had Jo been a man I would have fallen for her just the same.'

When I read for Beth that night I was convinced that the two were indeed soul mates. I had this extremely happy warm feeling about them both and the love they had for each other. But I also sensed that up until that moment Jo had been very unhappy. I knew, which Beth confirmed, that Jo's father had been schizophrenic, that her childhood had been very difficult and that learning to live with her father's identity problems had affected the way she thought about herself.

I advised Beth to stay calm and not to confront Jo, but to understand that she needed time and love to understand herself. Until Jo learnt to be happy with herself she could not expect to be happy with Beth or anyone else. Jo needed to be nurtured.

Some months ago Jo wrote to Beth to tell her that she would be returning to New York and that she wanted things to start again. She said she realized how much she loved Beth and I hope in time they will both know that they belong together.

Your soul, as I have said before, exists outside and beyond your physical form. When your soul mate is chosen for you, it is chosen for you because it is the right soul for you, not because of its sexuality. Just as a straight woman might fall for a blond man when they usually go for dark types, there is nothing to say that you might find yourself falling hopelessly in love with someone of the same sex. A woman who could not and would not accept her son's homosexuality asked me whether he would become heterosexual in spirit. 'I mean, they don't do that in the afterlife, do they, Rita?' she said disapprovingly. It may matter down here, it may be considered wrong by some, but in spirit it does not matter.

Whatever the situation try to be kind to all people involved. I used to read for a very lovely woman from London who was in her late thirties, married and had a couple of children at primary school. When she came for a reading one day I sensed something was not quite right and that her marriage was going to break up before the end of the year. Her spirit guide was telling me that an infidelity was taking place. He told me that it was with the couple's babysitter. Well, I have to say that I automatically assumed that it must be her husband who was having an affair with the babysitter, but when I mentioned the babysitter's name you should have seen the colour this lady's cheeks turned. It was she who was having the affair! It turned out that she and the babysitter had even fallen very deeply in love with each other. They were soul mates, and there was no question that she had to tell her husband and leave home. And though it broke her heart, she did so. She left her children with their father, although they spent weekends and holidays with her. She knew that it would be better for them to be with him. 'I must wait until they are old enough to understand,' she said. 'They have had enough disruption in their lives for the time being, I will tell them when the time is right for us all to be able to understand each other, and when they are old enough to know that I was not a bad person.'

KARMIC SOUL MATES

There is nothing to say that the relationship you have with a soul mate has to be consummated or sexual. It is possible to have a soul mate with whom you have a strictly platonic and non-romantic relationship. People have often come to me saying that their soul mate is their best friend and nothing more.

This kind of soul mate is someone with whom you have a special bond, a friendship based on a deep understanding of the other person. It could be a brother, sister, parent, cousin, or a close friend. But what differentiates this relationship from any other family tie or friendship is that there seems to be a spiritual link between you. You know how someone is feeling, you are both sensitive to each other's needs, there is an implicit trust between you. Whilst other people may not understand what you are going through, how you are feeling, or be able to communicate with you, you know that you can always rely on your karmic soul mate.

As I have said before, we all have a blueprint for our lives that sets out certain things which will happen to us. But this blueprint also holds certain people we are supposed to meet. These are people with whom we share a special bond. It is like being in a foreign country but finding someone who comes from the same place. You might meet someone with whom on the outside you have nothing in common. They may be wealthy while you are struggling; they maybe young, maybe single, while you are older and married. They may have come from a totally different world to yours – brought up in another country, not sharing any of your politics or beliefs – and yet there is something about this person, you have a link and a special bond with them that no one else can see or understand.

You may meet in a weird place and strike up conversation. suddenly, although you have known this person for five minutes, you feel closer to them than you ever have to your sister or to the best friend you have known all your life. With this person you can share many intimate details and thoughts – things you could never share with another soul. Why? Because your souls are similar.

I am talking about being more than just good friends. This is a very special spiritual understanding of another human being. Such people have been sent to you, just as your soul mate has (you can have both a soul mate and a karmic soul mate; you may also have one without the other). They are people who will help you through your life and whom you help back. You must always treasure friendships like these because they are rare and very special.

You may not see your karmic soul mate very often but when you do it is as though no time has passed at all. They will take you for who you are, just as the spirits do. Your karmic soul mate has great respect for you and never judges you, which is why they make good confidants. They allow for your mistakes, your shortcomings, and respect your differences of opinion.

Unlike the soul mate you are destined to be with, the bond between you two is not exclusive and you will not be paired together in the spirit world. You will go to your soul mate and they will go to theirs. Although there is no evidence to suggest any divinely inspired spiritual connection between karmic soul mates that does not mean that such a connection does not exist. I think that we are all destined to have a couple of karmic soul mates in our lives.

Just as a soul mate will bring something to our life, a karmic soul mate also has great influence over the course of our life. With these people we always have lessons to learn; they help shape us in some way. They evoke strong, intense feelings. However, we seldom develop a deep, long-term romantic relationship with them. Instead, they are there for us to grow with.

TWIN SOULS

Twins are spiritually linked from conception. Much has been written about the bond that exists between twins. We hear of how twins who, though separated at birth, lead parallel lives; how each can read the other's mind and how they can feel each other's pain. Twins often say that there is a 'psychic bond' between them, and that this is how, for example, they can sense when something bad is about to happen to the other.

The bond between twins is very much like the bond between soul mates. It is, after all, one that exists before our births and one which, I have found, transcends the grave. I find that the reading of twins, especially where one has passed over and the other is still alive, very strong. I can pick up if a person is a twin almost immediately. Twin souls find it very hard to live without each other and it is usual for a twin who has passed over actually to remain earthbound in order to be with his or her twin until they pass over.

But while the link is very tight between them, they are not soul mates as such because each has their own identity. Their souls may be very alike, making them spiritually close, but they are separate. I do not agree with the argument that they are split souls. Our souls are separate from our bodies. Even in the case of Siamese twins, it was meant to be that there were two lives and therefore two separate souls. Identical twins, who are not just physically but also mentally alike, will certainly have souls that are very similar, but again each is individual. Just because they have shared a womb does not mean that they share a soul.

Twins, just like the rest of us, have their own soul mates. It is even possible that they can become close or even closer to another soul other than their twin. The bond between the twins may be very strong and close but that does not mean they are incapable of knowing true love with another soul. It is, after all, a quite different kind of love.

COMPANION SOUL MATES

When we lose our soul mate either to the next life or down here, it is very hard. We only have one soul mate, it is true, but that is not to say that you cannot be in love more than once, or that you cannot have a good, wonderful relationship with another person here.

When your soul mate goes before you it can be very hard and very lonely. It does upset me to think of all those people out there who are suffering on their own. People who, because they have lost their mate, are now missing out on so many of the simple pleasures in life. Someone to share a meal with. Someone to take a holiday with. Someone to lock the door at night. Someone to kiss first thing in the morning.

Your soul mate in the spirit world would hate to think of you leading this kind of miserable life. They would not want you to be all by yourself, which is why they are not only happy when we find new companions, they encourage it. They would never be hurt or jealous because there are no such feelings in spirit. And what's more, they know how much you really love them. They know that you are soul mates, that you were destined to be together, and they know that even if you do remarry or start having feelings for another person, ultimately there is nothing to fear or be jealous of because they know the two of you will be together again.

I would be the first to encourage anyone here in this position to have another go, to be happy and to love again. People should not think for one instant that someone else could not bring them true and rewarding love. You should feel no guilt either. Your soul mate will not be jealous of you finding love down here, in fact they have probably not just encouraged this union but have even brought the two of you together. You should not feel guilty about the person with whom you have a second relationship either, because when they enter the spirit world they will be with their soul mate even if they have not found them on this plane.

When Bill and Catherine met they fell in love. She was a lot younger than he was but it didn't matter because they were soul mates. They spent two wonderful years together until suddenly Catherine died from a brain tumour. Bill was devastated, his world fell apart. He had never imagined that it would be Catherine who would be taken first. He didn't want to go on living.

Catherine and Bill had never married. They had been happy as they were; they thought that if they married it would have highlighted the difference in their ages. Nevertheless they were mad about each other. So when this happened Bill vowed he would never marry, that he would always be true to Catherine.

It must have been two years later that I read for Bill. I did not know about Catherine when he made the appointment but as soon as I read for him she came through. She said that she had never loved anyone in the way she loved him. She talked of what they did together, about their holidays. But she said that although she loved him, and that she would be waiting for him in spirit, he had to move on now.

She said she knew he had vowed not to marry anyone else, but he would. She knew because she was sending a lovely woman his way who would understand him. She said that the woman's initial was 'S', and that when he met her he would know it was her. She said that Charlie had helped her find this woman and that this would mean something to her. Bill hoped it would, because it meant nothing to him! He didn't know any Charlies neither here nor in spirit.

Eight months later Bill met a woman called Sylvia when he attended a book launch in London. A mutual friend introduced them. They got on well and had arranged to join some people for dinner after the party. At dinner Bill learnt that Sylvia had two children and had been widowed for five years. 'I'm so sorry, ' he said to her, 'I know how it feels.' 'What was his name?' he asked politely. 'Charlie,' she said.

I find that spirits can be quite conspiratorial when it comes to sorting out our love lives. They cannot bear to think of us alone and unhappy so they go out of their way to find someone for us.

This is why companion soul mates get on very easily with each other. They have after all been hand-picked for us by the person who loves us most, and this is also why we have them for life.

Because soul mates really do love us they don't mind us having another person in our lives for a while to keep us happy. Catherine and Charlie had obviously decided that if they worked together they could help both their soul mates at once. So Bill and Sylvia became companion soul mates, soul mates for this lifetime, if you like. They were in effect being 'lent' to each other by their own soul mates until the time when they would be reunited with their true eternal loves.

Afterword

Palms, Stars and Other Means of Finding Love

People often seem to be surprised that mediums can tell the identity of your soul mate before you have even met them yourself. We are able to do this because the spirit world already knows the identity of your soul mate and because the spiritual bond between soul mates is very strong. This is why it is easy to detect and why I am able to come out with the name of your soul mate early in a reading.

A good medium, and by that I mean someone with a genuine gift, should be able to help you with all matters of the heart. They are able to do this because your spirit guides should be able to tell them significant and important information about your past, present and your future.

Mediumship comes into being when innate psychic powers are developed in close cooperation with spirit guides. The guides are able to help the medium because of their advanced evolutionary state in spirit, and so act as tutors in these matters. A good medium will not only be clairvoyant (being able to see and interpret images) but also clairaudient, which means that they can hear voices from spirit guides and spirits in their 'inner' ear.

I say this because any information or advice you

receive from a medium should come from the spirit world and not the medium themselves. The medium is literally a channel. If the medium seems to know little about your spirits, about people in your family who have gone before you, then you should not take them too seriously when it comes to talking about your future and affairs of the heart. They may be wrong; the conditions may not be right for a good reading; a bad medium may be guessing.

Mediums should be specific. Most adults have lost a grandparent; to say 'I've got an elderly person up here' is not really good enough. A good medium should tell you something that no one else knows, because spirits do like to prove to you that it is in fact them. If it is your grandfather, for instance, he might tell you about how he used to take you to feed the ducks at the local pond when you were small. The medium may seem to offer trivial bits of information at first, but they are important, because it does actually prove that you are talking to a spirit.

I always say the information a medium gives should only ever be taken into consideration as guidance. You should not become dependent on mediums or lock yourself away waiting for destiny to knock on your door. You must live your life to the full.

And mediumship is not the only way of achieving psychic insight into a person's future. There are many different ways of reading a person, be it their past, their present or their future, without having direct contact with the spirit world. Palmistry, the crystal ball, Tarot readings, tea leaves, psychometry and horoscopes are all commonly used methods of determining one's destiny, and hence one's soul mate.

PALMISTRY

Palmistry is an ancient art. Fortune tellers say that your life and future may be read simply by looking at the formations of lines on your hand. They say you are able to tell a lot about a person from their hand because their palm is an intrinsic part of them. The way its lines form reflect your destiny. You can supposedly determine your life span, how many children and marriages you will have. Your palm can also tell you about your health and how prosperous you will be. I call the palm your life map. But while the palm, if read properly, can tell you things like this, it cannot go into more detail. It may tell you how many marriages you will have but it will not tell you if you are married, or will ever be married, to the right person. And you do not have to be a medium to read your palm. A book of palmistry can teach you the basics.

THE CRYSTAL BALL

If your palm is a life map then the crystal ball describes the journey that you will make in life. By reading the small stars of light reflected in a crystal ball the trained reader can determine what that journey has in store for you. When a person is given the ball and it is placed in their hand, the reader looks at the way the light interacts with these tiny stars. But like the palm it does not offer any specifics or details. A person who reads a crystal ball should also be clairvoyant, and be qualified in interpreting images and symbols.

Although I have my own crystal ball, which was left to me by my grandmother, Mary Alice, and has been passed down from my Romany ancestors, I do not like to use it in my work. For me the ball is just a focal point. I can get far more from listening to the voices in my 'inner' ear and looking at a person than I can staring at a thousand tiny stars within a piece of ancient glass.

TAROT

The Tarot is a set of traditional fortune telling cards that date back to the fourteenth century. There are seventy-eight cards in all, which are divided into two sets. The Minor Arcana has fifty-six cards, the Major Arcana has twenty-two. An allegorical figure is printed on each card and this holds a special meaning. The idea is that when the cards are shuffled by a person wanting to know their future, and then laid down by the reader of the cards, a map of one's past, present and future can be read in the interpretation of the symbols.

I am afraid that I am not a great believer in the power of the Tarot. If you have your Tarot cards read more than once the likelihood of you getting the same pattern of cards is tiny. This means that each time your future will be different, which doesn't add up to me.

TEA LEAVES

For years Romany gypsies have used tea leaves as a form of divination. By placing a cup of tea in the hand of the person you are reading for, by sipping the tea, then draining the liquid and swirling the cup in the hand, the reader can then examine the patterns the leaves have formed in the bottom of the cup. The reader then interprets these symbols. Like the ball, tea leaves simply provide a focal point for a reading. A truly gifted person should be able to know about your life just by being with you.

PSYCHOMETRY

It is possible to take an item of a person's belongings, hold it in your hand and tell something about the owner of the object from the piece. This is often practised with a piece of jewellery because it is worn close to you. I find psychometry useful, but its use is limited. It can only tell you about the owner or wearer of the jewellery themselves, and not the person who gave it to them or beyond.

THE ASTROLOGICAL CHART

The astrological chart is a useful guide to knowing about someone's life and their character. But as with any form of esoteric knowledge, including mediumship, you should not be governed by it. Like spiritualism, astrology is there to guide us, inform us and instruct us, but it should not dictate our every movement.

Our zodiac sign is relevant because the time at which we are born affects our emotional make-up. The moon controls the tides; it is therefore only logical that it would affect our wellbeing as individuals too. Each sign acts as a guide to discovering our emotional self, which is why I always ask for the star sign of a person before I read for them. I don't do this to guess their destiny (any information I give comes from the spirit world); I do it because it is a good guide, a thumbnail sketch, of emotional make-up. Knowing a person's star sign can help me gauge how they will take the information I am going to give them.

Knowing our own or our lover's date of birth is useful when looking at soul mates and how we will be together. But while we can look at the stars to see if we are astrologically compatible, this is a very general guide, and should never be used either to persuade or dissuade you from a type of person.

Your soul mate does not, after all, come astrologically guaranteed. You may find that your soul mate is opposite to you in astrological terms, but it should not mean that you walk away from them. You'll just have to take those characteristics into consideration. Use the stars as a guideline, work from there. If your partner's sign is prone to mood swings then be aware of it and learn to accept that, just as they in turn will learn how to deal with you. Learn to accept their personality traits, and remember that some are much stronger in certain people than they are in others of the same sign – if you want to get technical, ascendents and descendents also affect things. But as I say, don't become governed by these sorts of things. I have given a sketch here of the twelve signs of the zodiac.

ARIES (21 March–19 April)

Strong but sensitive
Birth Sign: Fire

Arians can be very stubborn, and you know when they have had a bad day. They are used to speaking their minds, which is good as you know where you stand with a partner born under this sign, but it can be difficult in a relationship. Be aware of the fact that they are incredibly possessive because they have to be secure. They are also prone to depression and feel terrible when a relationship breaks down. They make a good match with Leo.

TAURUS (20 April–20 May)

Strong, but I would be cautious with bad news
Birth sign: Earth

Those who are born under this sign tend to fall into two very separate camps: those who are born in April, and those born in May. The April Taureans are real 'mother earth' figures and put up with a lot. May ones are more creative, by and large, and like Gemini tend to fall in love with the idea of being in love. They are therefore late in finding their soul mate, whereas the April babies find them earlier. Both are very loyal people.

GEMINI (21 May–21 June)

Strong on the surface, but I would be wary of giving them bad news as they tend to worry
Birth sign: Air

Geminis can go through their lives without having a split. They are creative people, actors, for instance, hairdressers and artists. They carry their age well, and they are very happy once they meet their soul mate. But they do have to be careful that they don't fall in love with being in love.

CANCER (22 June–22 July)

Afraid of bad news
Birth Sign: Water

With Cancer, what they don't know won't hurt them. They try to appear strong, so many people might assume that Cancerians are strong, but in fact deep down they are very sensitive. Underneath their exterior they are afraid of most things. They have to be careful with their soul mate because they are jealous and possessive by nature. Cancerians adore people and being around others. They make great parents and they love their homes. Because Cancerians like people so much and have strong nesting instincts they make good nannies, cooks, or work well in any job that has to do with people or homes. They make good husbands and wives. Cancer goes well with Pisces, Virgo and Scorpio.

LEO (23 July–22 August)

Strong
Birth Sign: Fire

Leos like to be told that you love them all the time. They are good hard workers and they make good mothers. They are good at persevering. Leos are very possessive with their soul mates, so be careful! While in their minds it is OK for them to flirt around, it is not OK for their soul mate to do it. They go well with Aries.

VIRGO (23 August–22 September)

A little afraid of bad news
Birth Sign: Earth

Virgoans are very versatile. They tend to get on with most birth signs. They are very romantic and they are also perfectionists. Virgoans like to spend money and they have to watch that they don't live beyond their means. They tend to go for Librans, but in my experience this is not a very good match. I feel a water sign suits them best.

LIBRA (23 September–23 October)

Worries a lot
Birth Sign: Air

Librans are quiet by nature and are deep thinkers, especially those born in the month of September. They love animals and are extremely good workers. Librans tend to meet their soul mate late in life. They can be very stubborn. Librans like to surround themselves with nice things. They love to travel and they like uniforms. Libra is a good match for Sagittarius or Gemini.

SCORPIO (24 October–21 November)

Takes things very seriously
Birth Sign: Water

Scorpios are very attracted to other water signs but I do not recommend that a Scorpio fall for another Scorpio.

Scorpios find their soul mates usually between the ages of twenty and thirty. They like their freedom and independence, but once they find their soul mate they settle down. If they lose their soul mate it is very hard for them to find a substitute.

SAGITTARIUS (22 November–21 December)

Strong but sensitive
Birth Sign: Fire

Sagittarians are a lot like Capricorns; they usually marry late and are career-minded. They are actors. They cannot stand disloyalty, they are good workers. They are also very loyal and loving to their soul mate.

CAPRICORN (22 December–19 January)

Strong
Birth Sign: Earth

Capricorns love to achieve in life. I find that they are usually late in meeting their soul mate because their career has to come first. In the workplace, if they do not own their business, you will find that they are in charge of their office. Capricorns tend to be specialists, they like to know what they are doing – which is why they make good doctors, lawyers or pilots. In my experience they are very like Sagittarians, who are also very focused. These two signs also get on very well because they have so much in common and tend to have very similar interests. If a Capricorn marries young it tends not to work, for they are unlikely then to be with their soul mate. A Capricorn needs the time to grow and develop before they can even think of finding their soul mate.

AQUARIUS (20 January – 18 February)

I would be cautious with bad bews
Birth Sign: Air

Aquarians are dreamy people. They are only happy and committed to work when they are doing something that they enjoy. They find it difficult to make their minds up about things; even choosing an outfit to wear can be a task. They tend to dither, which leads to mistakes. Aquarians should always go for their first decision and follow their instincts. They love animals and grow very attached to people. They tend to lean on their partners, so losing a soul mate can be very difficult for an Aquarian, and they can feel very depressed or suicidal when this happens. Aquarians and Scorpios make good matches.

PISCES (19 February – 20 March)

I would be cautious with bad news
Birth Sign: Water

Pisceans can be very soft. Their eyes are their main feature, warm, striking and kind. They are very giving people, but they get very hurt by words. Money means nothing to Pisceans; happiness means far more. If they are not happy at work, they are not happy at home. They love their children, too. If a Piscean has a roof over their head and a meal on the table they are OK. They work well with Cancerians because they don't mind being told what to do.

A Final Word

Happy Endings

Whatever happens to you in this life, however bad things get, always remember that there is love out there for you. Love cannot stop tragedy, it cannot prevent death, cure illnesses or bring loved ones back to you, but it can ease the pain.

Even if we find love in this life we cannot guarantee that it will last our lifetime. But whatever happens to us, however lonely, sad or despairing we feel, we should know that we are all destined to have a happy ending. For whatever happens to us in this life, in the next life we will find true and eternal love.

RITA ROGERS

Mysteries

PAN BOOKS

Britain's most accurate and best-loved psychic explains the paranormal and supernatural.

In this book Rita talks about what it means to be psychic, where her gift comes from and how she uses her powers to help others. Rita examines subjects such as seances, Tarot, 'ghosts', premonitions, curses, hauntings and possessions.

Mysteries also details the numerous trails that Rita has followed in her life as a medium. This involves her work with the police and army, the murders she has helped families solve, and the missing people (dead or alive) she has located. She also talks about helping people find wills, money and objects and how she has saved lives by warning people against the actions they were about to take.

Following Rita's extraordinary career and reading her astonishing stories, the 'other' world no longer feels quite so far away.

RITA ROGERS

From One World to Another

PAN BOOKS

Rita Rogers inherited her gift, and a 400-year-old crystal ball, from her gypsy grandmother. But as more and more clients come to her from all over the world for readings, so do people seeking to understand her special gifts of communication with those who have 'passed over'.

From One World to Another attempts to explain these powers. It explores the strands of Rita Rogers' extraordinary life and her own philosophy of the spirit world, with first-hand accounts of remarkable encounters. Many of these are deeply moving, although Rita's inimitable personality also brings more than a touch of humour to some of these most astonishing true-life experiences.

Besides her very high-profile personal clients, Rita has also worked with the police. She has been involved in solving several well-known murder and child-abduction cases, and located the bodies of two missing soldiers in the Cairngorms.

Her unassuming approach and the authenticity of her findings will absorb readers, bringing a new understanding of these extraordinary powers, and even life itself.

JUSTINE PICARDIE

If the Spirit Moves You

PAN BOOKS

A memoir of life and love after death – poignant and sad as well as brave and uplifting.

In September 1997 Justine Picardie's sister, Ruth, died of breast cancer. Before she died, Ruth wrote a series of columns about her illness that were then published as the bestselling book, *Before I Say Goodbye.* In Justine's own remarkable book, Justine tells the story of life after death in a year in her own life after Ruth's death; and of a search for the afterlife in the age of reason, of scepticism, of science. It tells of the yearning for a voice in the silence, and of how we fill the space that appears when someone dies; or how the space fills itself.

'[*If the Spirit Moves You*] tackles some of the most important developments in psychic research during the twentieth century . . . The result is a book of great discipline, which uses the personal hell of bereavement as a way of investigating the limits of what we know about being both dead and alive'
Kathryn Hughes, *Daily Telegraph*

'It is the authenticity of Picardie's emotional quest, and her conclusions about life and love as much as death, that make this book so hopeful and engaging'
Harriet Griffey, *Financial Times*

RICHARD BACH

One

PAN BOOKS

A curious, loving fantasy in which Bach weaves science and spirit to explore concepts of time and self.

'What if we could talk face-to-face with the people we were in the past, with the people we are in parallel lifetimes, in alternate worlds? What would we tell them, and what would we ask? How would we change if we new what waits beyond space and time?'

In a journey with his wife, Leslie, Richard Bach travels to a realm where survival depends on discovering what the other aspects of themselves have learned on roads they never took; where imagination and fear are tools for saving worlds and destroying them; where dying is one step to overcoming death. *One* is Bach's most startling story yet, opening a mystical door on an alternative path to finding ourselves.

RICHARD BACH

A Gift of Wings

PAN BOOKS

Take flight with this collection of moving short stories from the author of Jonathan Livingston Seagull

These stories, inspired by Bach's lifelong passion for flight, filled with memories of friends from the past and friends not yet met, are woven together with warmth, honesty and courage. With signs and signals, coincidences and tangents turning up at every juncture, Bach shows how truly complex and beautiful life can be, and also how its troubles can in fact knock us onto better paths or teach us lessons we benefit from in other situations. Drawing on the allegorical power of flight, each a mini-parable, these stories will inspire you with their simple experiences made technicolour by the prism of Bach's extraordinary imagination.

Celebrating Richard Bach's unique vision, these transcend their pages to touch the real drama of life with magic that reaches out to us all across its limitless horizons.

RICHARD BACH

The Bridge Across Forever

PAN BOOKS

The search for love, glittering with Richard Bach's unique, prismatic imagination.

'Did you ever feel that you were missing someone you had never met?'

Haunted by the ghost of the wise, mystical, lovely lady who lives just around the corner in time, Richard Bach begins his quest to find her, to learn of love and immortality not in the hereafter, but in the here and now. Yet caught in storms of wealth and success, disaster and betrayal, he abandons the search, and the walls he builds for protection become his prison. Then he meets the one brilliant and beautiful woman who can set him free, and with her begins a transforming journey, a magical discovery of love and joy.

'None . . . can touch Richard Bach for his unerring ability to create beauty'
San Diego Tribune

RITA ROGERS

Learning to Live Again

PAN BOOKS

A Practical, Spiritual Guide to Coping with Bereavement

Grief is one of the strongest emotions that we face, arising as it does from the deep wells of love, affection and habit that tie us to one another. It is difficult to articulate the painful and often conflicting feelings that emerge from the various natural stages of grieving. But Rita Rogers, with her extraordinary gift for dealing with loss, can shine a light into that darkness, revealing that the people with whom we have shared love and friendship in this life can live on, albeit in another dimension, looking out for us and leading the way.

With compassion and understanding, Rita is our companion throughout the grieving process, reassuring us that even our most destructive and isolating feelings are part of a natural reaction. Addressing particular losses – of young and older children, of siblings, parents, friends, soul mates and those lost by suicide or in tragedies – Rita reaches across the divide of death, bringing the energy, the joy and the memories of those lost lives back into our broken hearts, and helping us all to learn to live again.

OTHER PAN BOOKS

AVAILABLE FROM PAN MACMILLAN

RITA ROGERS		
MYSTERIES	0 330 39079 1	£6.99
FROM ONE WORLD TO ANOTHER	0 330 36733 1	£6.99
LEARNING TO LIVE AGAIN	0 330 41285 X	£6.99
RICHARD BACH		
ONE	0 330 31173 5	£6.99
A GIFT OF WINGS	0 330 30421 6	£7.99
THE BRIDGE ACROSS FOREVER	0 330 29081 9	£6.99
JUSTINE PICARDIE		
IF THE SPIRIT MOVES YOU	0 330 48786 8	£7.99

All Pan Macmillan titles can be ordered from our website, www.panmacmillan.com, or from your local bookshop and are also available by post from:

Bookpost, PO Box 29, Douglas, Isle of Man IM99 1BQ
Credit cards accepted. For details:
Telephone: 01624 677237
Fax: 01624 670923
E-mail: bookshop@enterprise.net
www.bookpost.co.uk

Free postage and packing in the United Kingdom

Prices shown above were correct at the time of going to press. Pan Macmillan reserve the right to show new retail prices on covers which may differ from those previously advertised in the text or elsewhere.